Dear Ellie,
I have kept a calendar book for many years. I find writing special moments down better commits them to memory. Birthdays, births, anniversaries, graduations and also deaths.

Check it at the beginning of each month. Then remember those you love.

Much love,
Gran-gran Bryant
Christmas 2022

This Calendar Of
Special People, Important Dates And Amazing Memories
Belongs To:

_____

_____

Never forget an important date or the
memories that warrant an annual pause:
birthdays, anniversaries, deaths, baptisms,
graduations, a new job, a new house, retirement,
a first date, or a bucket list vacation.

Copyright © 2022 PaperTracks
All rights reserved. No part of this book can be
Copied or reproduced without written
Permission of the author.

## JANUARY 1

### BIRTHDAYS

| NAME | YEAR | NAME | YEAR |
|---|---|---|---|
|  |  |  |  |
|  |  |  |  |
|  |  |  |  |

### ANNIVERSARIES

| NAME | YEAR | NAME | YEAR |
|---|---|---|---|
|  |  |  |  |
|  |  |  |  |

### SPECIAL EVENTS & MEMORIES

| EVENT | YEAR | EVENT | YEAR |
|---|---|---|---|
|  |  |  |  |
|  |  |  |  |
|  |  |  |  |
|  |  |  |  |

## JANUARY 2

### BIRTHDAYS

| NAME | YEAR | NAME | YEAR |
|------|------|------|------|
|      |      |      |      |
|      |      |      |      |
|      |      |      |      |

### ANNIVERSARIES

| NAME | YEAR | NAME | YEAR |
|------|------|------|------|
|      |      |      |      |
|      |      |      |      |

### SPECIAL EVENTS & MEMORIES

| EVENT | YEAR | EVENT | YEAR |
|-------|------|-------|------|
|       |      |       |      |
|       |      |       |      |
|       |      |       |      |
|       |      |       |      |

## JANUARY 3

### BIRTHDAYS

| NAME | YEAR | NAME | YEAR |
|------|------|------|------|
|      |      |      |      |
|      |      |      |      |
|      |      |      |      |

### ANNIVERSARIES

| NAME | YEAR | NAME | YEAR |
|------|------|------|------|
|      |      |      |      |
|      |      |      |      |

### SPECIAL EVENTS & MEMORIES

| EVENT | YEAR | EVENT | YEAR |
|-------|------|-------|------|
|       |      |       |      |
|       |      |       |      |
|       |      |       |      |
|       |      |       |      |

## JANUARY 4

### BIRTHDAYS

| NAME | YEAR | NAME | YEAR |
|------|------|------|------|
|      |      |      |      |
|      |      |      |      |
|      |      |      |      |

### ANNIVERSARIES

| NAME | YEAR | NAME | YEAR |
|------|------|------|------|
|      |      |      |      |
|      |      |      |      |

### SPECIAL EVENTS & MEMORIES

| EVENT | YEAR | EVENT | YEAR |
|-------|------|-------|------|
|       |      |       |      |
|       |      |       |      |
|       |      |       |      |
|       |      |       |      |

## JANUARY 5

### BIRTHDAYS

| NAME | YEAR | NAME | YEAR |
|---|---|---|---|
|  |  |  |  |
|  |  |  |  |
|  |  |  |  |

### ANNIVERSARIES

| NAME | YEAR | NAME | YEAR |
|---|---|---|---|
|  |  |  |  |
|  |  |  |  |

### SPECIAL EVENTS & MEMORIES

| EVENT | YEAR | EVENT | YEAR |
|---|---|---|---|
|  |  |  |  |
|  |  |  |  |
|  |  |  |  |
|  |  |  |  |

## JANUARY 6

### BIRTHDAYS

| NAME | YEAR | NAME | YEAR |
|---|---|---|---|
| Angie Gavin |  |  |  |
|  |  |  |  |
|  |  |  |  |

### ANNIVERSARIES

| NAME | YEAR | NAME | YEAR |
|---|---|---|---|
|  |  |  |  |
|  |  |  |  |

### SPECIAL EVENTS & MEMORIES

| EVENT | YEAR | EVENT | YEAR |
|---|---|---|---|
|  |  |  |  |
|  |  |  |  |
|  |  |  |  |
|  |  |  |  |

## JANUARY 7

### BIRTHDAYS

| NAME | YEAR | NAME | YEAR |
|---|---|---|---|
|  |  |  |  |
|  |  |  |  |
|  |  |  |  |

### ANNIVERSARIES

| NAME | YEAR | NAME | YEAR |
|---|---|---|---|
|  |  |  |  |
|  |  |  |  |

### SPECIAL EVENTS & MEMORIES

| EVENT | YEAR | EVENT | YEAR |
|---|---|---|---|
|  |  |  |  |
|  |  |  |  |
|  |  |  |  |
|  |  |  |  |

## JANUARY 8

**BIRTHDAYS**

| NAME | YEAR | NAME | YEAR |
|---|---|---|---|
| Brandon Olszeski | | | |
| | | | |
| | | | |

**ANNIVERSARIES**

| NAME | YEAR | NAME | YEAR |
|---|---|---|---|
| | | | |
| | | | |

**SPECIAL EVENTS & MEMORIES**

| EVENT | YEAR | EVENT | YEAR |
|---|---|---|---|
| | | | |
| | | | |
| | | | |

## JANUARY 9

**BIRTHDAYS**

| NAME | YEAR | NAME | YEAR |
|---|---|---|---|
| | | | |
| | | | |
| | | | |

**ANNIVERSARIES**

| NAME | YEAR | NAME | YEAR |
|---|---|---|---|
| | | | |
| | | | |

**SPECIAL EVENTS & MEMORIES**

| EVENT | YEAR | EVENT | YEAR |
|---|---|---|---|
| | | | |
| | | | |
| | | | |

## JANUARY 10

**BIRTHDAYS**

| NAME | YEAR | NAME | YEAR |
|---|---|---|---|
| | | | |
| | | | |
| | | | |

**ANNIVERSARIES**

| NAME | YEAR | NAME | YEAR |
|---|---|---|---|
| | | | |
| | | | |

**SPECIAL EVENTS & MEMORIES**

| EVENT | YEAR | EVENT | YEAR |
|---|---|---|---|
| | | | |
| | | | |
| | | | |

# JANUARY 11

## BIRTHDAYS

| NAME | YEAR | NAME | YEAR |
|------|------|------|------|
|      |      |      |      |
|      |      |      |      |
|      |      |      |      |

## ANNIVERSARIES

| NAME | YEAR | NAME | YEAR |
|------|------|------|------|
|      |      |      |      |
|      |      |      |      |

## SPECIAL EVENTS & MEMORIES

| EVENT | YEAR | EVENT | YEAR |
|-------|------|-------|------|
|       |      |       |      |
|       |      |       |      |
|       |      |       |      |

# JANUARY 12

## BIRTHDAYS

| NAME | YEAR | NAME | YEAR |
|------|------|------|------|
|      |      |      |      |
|      |      |      |      |
|      |      |      |      |

## ANNIVERSARIES

| NAME | YEAR | NAME | YEAR |
|------|------|------|------|
|      |      |      |      |
|      |      |      |      |

## SPECIAL EVENTS & MEMORIES

| EVENT | YEAR | EVENT | YEAR |
|-------|------|-------|------|
|       |      |       |      |
|       |      |       |      |
|       |      |       |      |

# JANUARY 13

## BIRTHDAYS

| NAME | YEAR | NAME | YEAR |
|------|------|------|------|
|      |      |      |      |
|      |      |      |      |
|      |      |      |      |

## ANNIVERSARIES

| NAME | YEAR | NAME | YEAR |
|------|------|------|------|
|      |      |      |      |
|      |      |      |      |

## SPECIAL EVENTS & MEMORIES

| EVENT | YEAR | EVENT | YEAR |
|-------|------|-------|------|
|       |      |       |      |
|       |      |       |      |
|       |      |       |      |

## JANUARY 14

**BIRTHDAYS**

| NAME | YEAR | NAME | YEAR |
|---|---|---|---|
| | | | |
| | | | |
| | | | |

**ANNIVERSARIES**

| NAME | YEAR | NAME | YEAR |
|---|---|---|---|
| | | | |
| | | | |

**SPECIAL EVENTS & MEMORIES**

| EVENT | YEAR | EVENT | YEAR |
|---|---|---|---|
| | | | |
| | | | |
| | | | |
| | | | |

## JANUARY 15

**BIRTHDAYS**

| NAME | YEAR | NAME | YEAR |
|---|---|---|---|
| | | | |
| | | | |
| | | | |

**ANNIVERSARIES**

| NAME | YEAR | NAME | YEAR |
|---|---|---|---|
| | | | |
| | | | |

**SPECIAL EVENTS & MEMORIES**

| EVENT | YEAR | EVENT | YEAR |
|---|---|---|---|
| | | | |
| | | | |
| | | | |
| | | | |

## JANUARY 16

**BIRTHDAYS**

| NAME | YEAR | NAME | YEAR |
|---|---|---|---|
| | | | |
| | | | |
| | | | |

**ANNIVERSARIES**

| NAME | YEAR | NAME | YEAR |
|---|---|---|---|
| | | | |
| | | | |

**SPECIAL EVENTS & MEMORIES**

| EVENT | YEAR | EVENT | YEAR |
|---|---|---|---|
| | | | |
| | | | |
| | | | |
| | | | |

## JANUARY 17

### BIRTHDAYS

| NAME | YEAR | NAME | YEAR |
|---|---|---|---|
|  |  |  |  |
|  |  |  |  |
|  |  |  |  |

### ANNIVERSARIES

| NAME | YEAR | NAME | YEAR |
|---|---|---|---|
|  |  |  |  |
|  |  |  |  |

### SPECIAL EVENTS & MEMORIES

| EVENT | YEAR | EVENT | YEAR |
|---|---|---|---|
|  |  |  |  |
|  |  |  |  |
|  |  |  |  |

## JANUARY 18

### BIRTHDAYS

| NAME | YEAR | NAME | YEAR |
|---|---|---|---|
|  |  |  |  |
|  |  |  |  |
|  |  |  |  |

### ANNIVERSARIES

| NAME | YEAR | NAME | YEAR |
|---|---|---|---|
|  |  |  |  |
|  |  |  |  |

### SPECIAL EVENTS & MEMORIES

| EVENT | YEAR | EVENT | YEAR |
|---|---|---|---|
|  |  |  |  |
|  |  |  |  |
|  |  |  |  |

## JANUARY 19

### BIRTHDAYS

| NAME | YEAR | NAME | YEAR |
|---|---|---|---|
| Layne | 2000 |  |  |
|  |  |  |  |
|  |  |  |  |

### ANNIVERSARIES

| NAME | YEAR | NAME | YEAR |
|---|---|---|---|
|  |  |  |  |
|  |  |  |  |

### SPECIAL EVENTS & MEMORIES

| EVENT | YEAR | EVENT | YEAR |
|---|---|---|---|
|  |  |  |  |
|  |  |  |  |
|  |  |  |  |

## JANUARY 20

**BIRTHDAYS**

| NAME | YEAR | NAME | YEAR |
|---|---|---|---|
| | | | |
| | | | |
| | | | |

**ANNIVERSARIES**

| NAME | YEAR | NAME | YEAR |
|---|---|---|---|
| | | | |
| | | | |

**SPECIAL EVENTS & MEMORIES**

| EVENT | YEAR | EVENT | YEAR |
|---|---|---|---|
| | | | |
| | | | |
| | | | |

## JANUARY 21

**BIRTHDAYS**

| NAME | YEAR | NAME | YEAR |
|---|---|---|---|
| | | | |
| | | | |
| | | | |

**ANNIVERSARIES**

| NAME | YEAR | NAME | YEAR |
|---|---|---|---|
| | | | |
| | | | |

**SPECIAL EVENTS & MEMORIES**

| EVENT | YEAR | EVENT | YEAR |
|---|---|---|---|
| | | | |
| | | | |
| | | | |

## JANUARY 22

**BIRTHDAYS**

| NAME | YEAR | NAME | YEAR |
|---|---|---|---|
| | | | |
| | | | |
| | | | |

**ANNIVERSARIES**

| NAME | YEAR | NAME | YEAR |
|---|---|---|---|
| | | | |
| | | | |

**SPECIAL EVENTS & MEMORIES**

| EVENT | YEAR | EVENT | YEAR |
|---|---|---|---|
| | | | |
| | | | |
| | | | |

# JANUARY 23

## BIRTHDAYS
| NAME | YEAR | NAME | YEAR |
|---|---|---|---|
|  |  |  |  |
|  |  |  |  |
|  |  |  |  |

## ANNIVERSARIES
| NAME | YEAR | NAME | YEAR |
|---|---|---|---|
|  |  |  |  |
|  |  |  |  |

## SPECIAL EVENTS & MEMORIES
| EVENT | YEAR | EVENT | YEAR |
|---|---|---|---|
|  |  |  |  |
|  |  |  |  |
|  |  |  |  |
|  |  |  |  |

# JANUARY 24

## BIRTHDAYS
| NAME | YEAR | NAME | YEAR |
|---|---|---|---|
|  |  |  |  |
|  |  |  |  |
|  |  |  |  |

## ANNIVERSARIES
| NAME | YEAR | NAME | YEAR |
|---|---|---|---|
|  |  |  |  |
|  |  |  |  |

## SPECIAL EVENTS & MEMORIES
| EVENT | YEAR | EVENT | YEAR |
|---|---|---|---|
|  |  |  |  |
|  |  |  |  |
|  |  |  |  |
|  |  |  |  |

# JANUARY 25

## BIRTHDAYS
| NAME | YEAR | NAME | YEAR |
|---|---|---|---|
|  |  |  |  |
|  |  |  |  |
|  |  |  |  |

## ANNIVERSARIES
| NAME | YEAR | NAME | YEAR |
|---|---|---|---|
|  |  |  |  |
|  |  |  |  |

## SPECIAL EVENTS & MEMORIES
| EVENT | YEAR | EVENT | YEAR |
|---|---|---|---|
|  |  |  |  |
|  |  |  |  |
|  |  |  |  |
|  |  |  |  |

## JANUARY 26

**BIRTHDAYS**

| NAME | YEAR | NAME | YEAR |
|---|---|---|---|
|  |  |  |  |
|  |  |  |  |

**ANNIVERSARIES**

| NAME | YEAR | NAME | YEAR |
|---|---|---|---|
|  |  |  |  |
|  |  |  |  |

**SPECIAL EVENTS & MEMORIES**

| EVENT | YEAR | EVENT | YEAR |
|---|---|---|---|
|  |  |  |  |
|  |  |  |  |
|  |  |  |  |

## JANUARY 27

**BIRTHDAYS**

| NAME | YEAR | NAME | YEAR |
|---|---|---|---|
|  |  |  |  |
|  |  |  |  |

**ANNIVERSARIES**

| NAME | YEAR | NAME | YEAR |
|---|---|---|---|
|  |  |  |  |
|  |  |  |  |

**SPECIAL EVENTS & MEMORIES**

| EVENT | YEAR | EVENT | YEAR |
|---|---|---|---|
|  |  |  |  |
|  |  |  |  |
|  |  |  |  |

## JANUARY 28

**BIRTHDAYS**

| NAME | YEAR | NAME | YEAR |
|---|---|---|---|
| Barry Huff |  |  |  |
|  |  |  |  |

**ANNIVERSARIES**

| NAME | YEAR | NAME | YEAR |
|---|---|---|---|
| Parker + Rebekah | 2023 |  |  |
|  |  |  |  |

**SPECIAL EVENTS & MEMORIES**

| EVENT | YEAR | EVENT | YEAR |
|---|---|---|---|
|  |  |  |  |
|  |  |  |  |
|  |  |  |  |

## JANUARY 29

### BIRTHDAYS

| NAME | YEAR | NAME | YEAR |
|---|---|---|---|
| | | | |
| | | | |
| | | | |

### ANNIVERSARIES

| NAME | YEAR | NAME | YEAR |
|---|---|---|---|
| | | | |
| | | | |

### SPECIAL EVENTS & MEMORIES

| EVENT | YEAR | EVENT | YEAR |
|---|---|---|---|
| | | | |
| | | | |
| | | | |
| | | | |

## JANUARY 30

### BIRTHDAYS

| NAME | YEAR | NAME | YEAR |
|---|---|---|---|
| | | | |
| | | | |
| | | | |

### ANNIVERSARIES

| NAME | YEAR | NAME | YEAR |
|---|---|---|---|
| | | | |
| | | | |

### SPECIAL EVENTS & MEMORIES

| EVENT | YEAR | EVENT | YEAR |
|---|---|---|---|
| | | | |
| | | | |
| | | | |
| | | | |

## JANUARY 31

### BIRTHDAYS

| NAME | YEAR | NAME | YEAR |
|---|---|---|---|
| | | | |
| | | | |
| | | | |

### ANNIVERSARIES

| NAME | YEAR | NAME | YEAR |
|---|---|---|---|
| | | | |
| | | | |

### SPECIAL EVENTS & MEMORIES

| EVENT | YEAR | EVENT | YEAR |
|---|---|---|---|
| | | | |
| | | | |
| | | | |
| | | | |

# FEBRUARY 1

### BIRTHDAYS

| NAME | YEAR | NAME | YEAR |
|------|------|------|------|
|      |      |      |      |
|      |      |      |      |
|      |      |      |      |

### ANNIVERSARIES

| NAME | YEAR | NAME | YEAR |
|------|------|------|------|
|      |      |      |      |
|      |      |      |      |

### SPECIAL EVENTS & MEMORIES

| EVENT | YEAR | EVENT | YEAR |
|-------|------|-------|------|
|       |      |       |      |
|       |      |       |      |
|       |      |       |      |
|       |      |       |      |

# FEBRUARY 2

### BIRTHDAYS

| NAME | YEAR | NAME | YEAR |
|------|------|------|------|
|      |      |      |      |
|      |      |      |      |
|      |      |      |      |

### ANNIVERSARIES

| NAME | YEAR | NAME | YEAR |
|------|------|------|------|
|      |      |      |      |
|      |      |      |      |

### SPECIAL EVENTS & MEMORIES

| EVENT | YEAR | EVENT | YEAR |
|-------|------|-------|------|
|       |      |       |      |
|       |      |       |      |
|       |      |       |      |
|       |      |       |      |

# FEBRUARY 3

### BIRTHDAYS

| NAME | YEAR | NAME | YEAR |
|---|---|---|---|
|  |  |  |  |
|  |  |  |  |
|  |  |  |  |

### ANNIVERSARIES

| NAME | YEAR | NAME | YEAR |
|---|---|---|---|
|  |  |  |  |
|  |  |  |  |

### SPECIAL EVENTS & MEMORIES

| EVENT | YEAR | EVENT | YEAR |
|---|---|---|---|
|  |  |  |  |
|  |  |  |  |
|  |  |  |  |
|  |  |  |  |

# FEBRUARY 4

### BIRTHDAYS

| NAME | YEAR | NAME | YEAR |
|---|---|---|---|
|  |  |  |  |
|  |  |  |  |
|  |  |  |  |

### ANNIVERSARIES

| NAME | YEAR | NAME | YEAR |
|---|---|---|---|
|  |  |  |  |
|  |  |  |  |

### SPECIAL EVENTS & MEMORIES

| EVENT | YEAR | EVENT | YEAR |
|---|---|---|---|
|  |  |  |  |
|  |  |  |  |
|  |  |  |  |
|  |  |  |  |

# FEBRUARY 5

### BIRTHDAYS

| NAME | YEAR | NAME | YEAR |
|---|---|---|---|
|  |  |  |  |
|  |  |  |  |
|  |  |  |  |

### ANNIVERSARIES

| NAME | YEAR | NAME | YEAR |
|---|---|---|---|
|  |  |  |  |
|  |  |  |  |

### SPECIAL EVENTS & MEMORIES

| EVENT | YEAR | EVENT | YEAR |
|---|---|---|---|
|  |  |  |  |
|  |  |  |  |
|  |  |  |  |
|  |  |  |  |

## FEBRUARY 6

### BIRTHDAYS
| NAME | YEAR | NAME | YEAR |
|---|---|---|---|
| | | | |
| | | | |
| | | | |

### ANNIVERSARIES
| NAME | YEAR | NAME | YEAR |
|---|---|---|---|
| | | | |
| | | | |

### SPECIAL EVENTS & MEMORIES
| EVENT | YEAR | EVENT | YEAR |
|---|---|---|---|
| | | | |
| | | | |
| | | | |
| | | | |

## FEBRUARY 7

### BIRTHDAYS
| NAME | YEAR | NAME | YEAR |
|---|---|---|---|
| | | | |
| | | | |
| | | | |

### ANNIVERSARIES
| NAME | YEAR | NAME | YEAR |
|---|---|---|---|
| | | | |
| | | | |

### SPECIAL EVENTS & MEMORIES
| EVENT | YEAR | EVENT | YEAR |
|---|---|---|---|
| | | | |
| | | | |
| | | | |
| | | | |

## FEBRUARY 8

### BIRTHDAYS
| NAME | YEAR | NAME | YEAR |
|---|---|---|---|
| | | | |
| | | | |
| | | | |

### ANNIVERSARIES
| NAME | YEAR | NAME | YEAR |
|---|---|---|---|
| | | | |
| | | | |

### SPECIAL EVENTS & MEMORIES
| EVENT | YEAR | EVENT | YEAR |
|---|---|---|---|
| | | | |
| | | | |
| | | | |
| | | | |

## FEBRUARY 9

**BIRTHDAYS**

| NAME | YEAR | NAME | YEAR |
|------|------|------|------|
|      |      |      |      |
|      |      |      |      |

**ANNIVERSARIES**

| NAME | YEAR | NAME | YEAR |
|------|------|------|------|
|      |      |      |      |
|      |      |      |      |

**SPECIAL EVENTS & MEMORIES**

| EVENT | YEAR | EVENT | YEAR |
|-------|------|-------|------|
|       |      |       |      |
|       |      |       |      |
|       |      |       |      |

## FEBRUARY 10

**BIRTHDAYS**

| NAME | YEAR | NAME | YEAR |
|------|------|------|------|
|      |      |      |      |
|      |      |      |      |

**ANNIVERSARIES**

| NAME | YEAR | NAME | YEAR |
|------|------|------|------|
|      |      |      |      |
|      |      |      |      |

**SPECIAL EVENTS & MEMORIES**

| EVENT | YEAR | EVENT | YEAR |
|-------|------|-------|------|
|       |      |       |      |
|       |      |       |      |
|       |      |       |      |

## FEBRUARY 11

**BIRTHDAYS**

| NAME | YEAR | NAME | YEAR |
|------|------|------|------|
|      |      |      |      |
|      |      |      |      |

**ANNIVERSARIES**

| NAME | YEAR | NAME | YEAR |
|------|------|------|------|
|      |      |      |      |
|      |      |      |      |

**SPECIAL EVENTS & MEMORIES**

| EVENT | YEAR | EVENT | YEAR |
|-------|------|-------|------|
|       |      |       |      |
|       |      |       |      |
|       |      |       |      |

## FEBRUARY 12

### BIRTHDAYS
| NAME | YEAR | NAME | YEAR |
|---|---|---|---|
|  |  |  |  |
|  |  |  |  |
|  |  |  |  |

### ANNIVERSARIES
| NAME | YEAR | NAME | YEAR |
|---|---|---|---|
|  |  |  |  |
|  |  |  |  |

### SPECIAL EVENTS & MEMORIES
| EVENT | YEAR | EVENT | YEAR |
|---|---|---|---|
|  |  |  |  |
|  |  |  |  |
|  |  |  |  |
|  |  |  |  |

## FEBRUARY 13

### BIRTHDAYS
| NAME | YEAR | NAME | YEAR |
|---|---|---|---|
|  |  |  |  |
|  |  |  |  |
|  |  |  |  |

### ANNIVERSARIES
| NAME | YEAR | NAME | YEAR |
|---|---|---|---|
|  |  |  |  |
|  |  |  |  |

### SPECIAL EVENTS & MEMORIES
| EVENT | YEAR | EVENT | YEAR |
|---|---|---|---|
|  |  |  |  |
|  |  |  |  |
|  |  |  |  |
|  |  |  |  |

## FEBRUARY 14

### BIRTHDAYS
| NAME | YEAR | NAME | YEAR |
|---|---|---|---|
|  |  |  |  |
|  |  |  |  |
|  |  |  |  |

### ANNIVERSARIES
| NAME | YEAR | NAME | YEAR |
|---|---|---|---|
|  |  |  |  |
|  |  |  |  |

### SPECIAL EVENTS & MEMORIES
| EVENT | YEAR | EVENT | YEAR |
|---|---|---|---|
|  |  |  |  |
|  |  |  |  |
|  |  |  |  |
|  |  |  |  |

# FEBRUARY 15

**BIRTHDAYS**

| NAME | YEAR | NAME | YEAR |
|---|---|---|---|
| | | | |
| | | | |
| | | | |

**ANNIVERSARIES**

| NAME | YEAR | NAME | YEAR |
|---|---|---|---|
| | | | |
| | | | |

**SPECIAL EVENTS & MEMORIES**

| EVENT | YEAR | EVENT | YEAR |
|---|---|---|---|
| | | | |
| | | | |
| | | | |
| | | | |

# FEBRUARY 16

**BIRTHDAYS**

| NAME | YEAR | NAME | YEAR |
|---|---|---|---|
| | | | |
| | | | |
| | | | |

**ANNIVERSARIES**

| NAME | YEAR | NAME | YEAR |
|---|---|---|---|
| | | | |
| | | | |

**SPECIAL EVENTS & MEMORIES**

| EVENT | YEAR | EVENT | YEAR |
|---|---|---|---|
| | | | |
| | | | |
| | | | |
| | | | |

# FEBRUARY 17

**BIRTHDAYS**

| NAME | YEAR | NAME | YEAR |
|---|---|---|---|
| | | | |
| | | | |
| | | | |

**ANNIVERSARIES**

| NAME | YEAR | NAME | YEAR |
|---|---|---|---|
| | | | |
| | | | |

**SPECIAL EVENTS & MEMORIES**

| EVENT | YEAR | EVENT | YEAR |
|---|---|---|---|
| | | | |
| | | | |
| | | | |
| | | | |

# FEBRUARY 18

## BIRTHDAYS

| NAME | YEAR | NAME | YEAR |
|---|---|---|---|
| | | | |
| | | | |
| | | | |

## ANNIVERSARIES

| NAME | YEAR | NAME | YEAR |
|---|---|---|---|
| | | | |
| | | | |

## SPECIAL EVENTS & MEMORIES

| EVENT | YEAR | EVENT | YEAR |
|---|---|---|---|
| | | | |
| | | | |
| | | | |

# FEBRUARY 19

## BIRTHDAYS

| NAME | YEAR | NAME | YEAR |
|---|---|---|---|
| Stacy Harris ♥ | 1966 | | |
| | | | |
| | | | |

## ANNIVERSARIES

| NAME | YEAR | NAME | YEAR |
|---|---|---|---|
| | | | |
| | | | |

## SPECIAL EVENTS & MEMORIES

| EVENT | YEAR | EVENT | YEAR |
|---|---|---|---|
| | | | |
| | | | |
| | | | |

# FEBRUARY 20

## BIRTHDAYS

| NAME | YEAR | NAME | YEAR |
|---|---|---|---|
| | | | |
| | | | |
| | | | |

## ANNIVERSARIES

| NAME | YEAR | NAME | YEAR |
|---|---|---|---|
| | | | |
| | | | |

## SPECIAL EVENTS & MEMORIES

| EVENT | YEAR | EVENT | YEAR |
|---|---|---|---|
| | | | |
| | | | |
| | | | |

## FEBRUARY 21

**BIRTHDAYS**

| NAME | YEAR | NAME | YEAR |
|---|---|---|---|
| | | | |
| | | | |
| | | | |

**ANNIVERSARIES**

| NAME | YEAR | NAME | YEAR |
|---|---|---|---|
| | | | |
| | | | |

**SPECIAL EVENTS & MEMORIES**

| EVENT | YEAR | EVENT | YEAR |
|---|---|---|---|
| | | | |
| | | | |
| | | | |
| | | | |

## FEBRUARY 22

**BIRTHDAYS**

| NAME | YEAR | NAME | YEAR |
|---|---|---|---|
| | | | |
| | | | |
| | | | |

**ANNIVERSARIES**

| NAME | YEAR | NAME | YEAR |
|---|---|---|---|
| | | | |
| | | | |

**SPECIAL EVENTS & MEMORIES**

| EVENT | YEAR | EVENT | YEAR |
|---|---|---|---|
| | | | |
| | | | |
| | | | |
| | | | |

## FEBRUARY 23

**BIRTHDAYS**

| NAME | YEAR | NAME | YEAR |
|---|---|---|---|
| | | | |
| | | | |
| | | | |

**ANNIVERSARIES**

| NAME | YEAR | NAME | YEAR |
|---|---|---|---|
| | | | |
| | | | |

**SPECIAL EVENTS & MEMORIES**

| EVENT | YEAR | EVENT | YEAR |
|---|---|---|---|
| | | | |
| | | | |
| | | | |
| | | | |

## FEBRUARY 24

### BIRTHDAYS

| NAME | YEAR | NAME | YEAR |
|---|---|---|---|
| | | | |
| | | | |
| | | | |

### ANNIVERSARIES

| NAME | YEAR | NAME | YEAR |
|---|---|---|---|
| | | | |
| | | | |

### SPECIAL EVENTS & MEMORIES

| EVENT | YEAR | EVENT | YEAR |
|---|---|---|---|
| | | | |
| | | | |
| | | | |
| | | | |

## FEBRUARY 25

### BIRTHDAYS

| NAME | YEAR | NAME | YEAR |
|---|---|---|---|
| | | | |
| | | | |
| | | | |

### ANNIVERSARIES

| NAME | YEAR | NAME | YEAR |
|---|---|---|---|
| | | | |
| | | | |

### SPECIAL EVENTS & MEMORIES

| EVENT | YEAR | EVENT | YEAR |
|---|---|---|---|
| | | | |
| | | | |
| | | | |
| | | | |

## FEBRUARY 26

### BIRTHDAYS

| NAME | YEAR | NAME | YEAR |
|---|---|---|---|
| | | | |
| | | | |
| | | | |

### ANNIVERSARIES

| NAME | YEAR | NAME | YEAR |
|---|---|---|---|
| | | | |
| | | | |

### SPECIAL EVENTS & MEMORIES

| EVENT | YEAR | EVENT | YEAR |
|---|---|---|---|
| | | | |
| | | | |
| | | | |
| | | | |

## FEBRUARY 27

### BIRTHDAYS

| NAME | YEAR | NAME | YEAR |
|---|---|---|---|
|  |  |  |  |
|  |  |  |  |

### ANNIVERSARIES

| NAME | YEAR | NAME | YEAR |
|---|---|---|---|
|  |  |  |  |

### SPECIAL EVENTS & MEMORIES

| EVENT | YEAR | EVENT | YEAR |
|---|---|---|---|
|  |  |  |  |
|  |  |  |  |
|  |  |  |  |

## FEBRUARY 28

### BIRTHDAYS

| NAME | YEAR | NAME | YEAR |
|---|---|---|---|
|  |  |  |  |
|  |  |  |  |

### ANNIVERSARIES

| NAME | YEAR | NAME | YEAR |
|---|---|---|---|
|  |  |  |  |

### SPECIAL EVENTS & MEMORIES

| EVENT | YEAR | EVENT | YEAR |
|---|---|---|---|
|  |  |  |  |
|  |  |  |  |
|  |  |  |  |

## FEBRUARY 29

### BIRTHDAYS

| NAME | YEAR | NAME | YEAR |
|---|---|---|---|
|  |  |  |  |
|  |  |  |  |

### ANNIVERSARIES

| NAME | YEAR | NAME | YEAR |
|---|---|---|---|
|  |  |  |  |

### SPECIAL EVENTS & MEMORIES

| EVENT | YEAR | EVENT | YEAR |
|---|---|---|---|
|  |  |  |  |
|  |  |  |  |
|  |  |  |  |

# MARCH

*" A friend loves at all times "*
Proverbs 17:17

## MARCH 1

### BIRTHDAYS
| NAME | YEAR | NAME | YEAR |
|---|---|---|---|
|  |  |  |  |
|  |  |  |  |
|  |  |  |  |

### ANNIVERSARIES
| NAME | YEAR | NAME | YEAR |
|---|---|---|---|
|  |  |  |  |
|  |  |  |  |

### SPECIAL EVENTS & MEMORIES
| EVENT | YEAR | EVENT | YEAR |
|---|---|---|---|
|  |  |  |  |
|  |  |  |  |
|  |  |  |  |
|  |  |  |  |

# MARCH 2

## BIRTHDAYS

| NAME | YEAR | NAME | YEAR |
|------|------|------|------|
|      |      |      |      |
|      |      |      |      |

## ANNIVERSARIES

| NAME | YEAR | NAME | YEAR |
|------|------|------|------|
|      |      |      |      |
|      |      |      |      |

## SPECIAL EVENTS & MEMORIES

| EVENT | YEAR | EVENT | YEAR |
|-------|------|-------|------|
|       |      |       |      |
|       |      |       |      |
|       |      |       |      |

# MARCH 3

## BIRTHDAYS

| NAME | YEAR | NAME | YEAR |
|------|------|------|------|
|      |      |      |      |
|      |      |      |      |
|      |      |      |      |

## ANNIVERSARIES

| NAME | YEAR | NAME | YEAR |
|------|------|------|------|
|      |      |      |      |
|      |      |      |      |

## SPECIAL EVENTS & MEMORIES

| EVENT | YEAR | EVENT | YEAR |
|-------|------|-------|------|
|       |      |       |      |
|       |      |       |      |
|       |      |       |      |

# MARCH 4

## BIRTHDAYS

| NAME | YEAR | NAME | YEAR |
|------|------|------|------|
|      |      |      |      |
|      |      |      |      |
|      |      |      |      |

## ANNIVERSARIES

| NAME | YEAR | NAME | YEAR |
|------|------|------|------|
|      |      |      |      |
|      |      |      |      |

## SPECIAL EVENTS & MEMORIES

| EVENT | YEAR | EVENT | YEAR |
|-------|------|-------|------|
|       |      |       |      |
|       |      |       |      |
|       |      |       |      |

## MARCH 5

### BIRTHDAYS
| NAME | YEAR | NAME | YEAR |
|------|------|------|------|
|      |      |      |      |
|      |      |      |      |
|      |      |      |      |

### ANNIVERSARIES
| NAME | YEAR | NAME | YEAR |
|------|------|------|------|
|      |      |      |      |
|      |      |      |      |

### SPECIAL EVENTS & MEMORIES
| EVENT | YEAR | EVENT | YEAR |
|-------|------|-------|------|
|       |      |       |      |
|       |      |       |      |
|       |      |       |      |
|       |      |       |      |

## MARCH 6

### BIRTHDAYS
| NAME | YEAR | NAME | YEAR |
|------|------|------|------|
|      |      |      |      |
|      |      |      |      |
|      |      |      |      |

### ANNIVERSARIES
| NAME | YEAR | NAME | YEAR |
|------|------|------|------|
|      |      |      |      |
|      |      |      |      |

### SPECIAL EVENTS & MEMORIES
| EVENT | YEAR | EVENT | YEAR |
|-------|------|-------|------|
|       |      |       |      |
|       |      |       |      |
|       |      |       |      |
|       |      |       |      |

## MARCH 7

### BIRTHDAYS
| NAME | YEAR | NAME | YEAR |
|------|------|------|------|
|      |      |      |      |
|      |      |      |      |
|      |      |      |      |

### ANNIVERSARIES
| NAME | YEAR | NAME | YEAR |
|------|------|------|------|
|      |      |      |      |
|      |      |      |      |

### SPECIAL EVENTS & MEMORIES
| EVENT | YEAR | EVENT | YEAR |
|-------|------|-------|------|
|       |      |       |      |
|       |      |       |      |
|       |      |       |      |
|       |      |       |      |

## MARCH 8

**BIRTHDAYS**

| NAME | YEAR | NAME | YEAR |
|---|---|---|---|
| | | | |
| | | | |
| | | | |

**ANNIVERSARIES**

| NAME | YEAR | NAME | YEAR |
|---|---|---|---|
| | | | |
| | | | |

**SPECIAL EVENTS & MEMORIES**

| EVENT | YEAR | EVENT | YEAR |
|---|---|---|---|
| | | | |
| | | | |
| | | | |

## MARCH 9

**BIRTHDAYS**

| NAME | YEAR | NAME | YEAR |
|---|---|---|---|
| | | | |
| | | | |
| | | | |

**ANNIVERSARIES**

| NAME | YEAR | NAME | YEAR |
|---|---|---|---|
| | | | |
| | | | |

**SPECIAL EVENTS & MEMORIES**

| EVENT | YEAR | EVENT | YEAR |
|---|---|---|---|
| | | | |
| | | | |
| | | | |

## MARCH 10

**BIRTHDAYS**

| NAME | YEAR | NAME | YEAR |
|---|---|---|---|
| | | | |
| | | | |
| | | | |

**ANNIVERSARIES**

| NAME | YEAR | NAME | YEAR |
|---|---|---|---|
| | | | |
| | | | |

**SPECIAL EVENTS & MEMORIES**

| EVENT | YEAR | EVENT | YEAR |
|---|---|---|---|
| | | | |
| | | | |
| | | | |

# MARCH 11

## BIRTHDAYS
| NAME | YEAR | NAME | YEAR |
|---|---|---|---|
|  |  |  |  |
|  |  |  |  |

## ANNIVERSARIES
| NAME | YEAR | NAME | YEAR |
|---|---|---|---|
|  |  |  |  |
|  |  |  |  |

## SPECIAL EVENTS & MEMORIES
| EVENT | YEAR | EVENT | YEAR |
|---|---|---|---|
|  |  |  |  |
|  |  |  |  |
|  |  |  |  |

# MARCH 12

## BIRTHDAYS
| NAME | YEAR | NAME | YEAR |
|---|---|---|---|
|  |  |  |  |
|  |  |  |  |

## ANNIVERSARIES
| NAME | YEAR | NAME | YEAR |
|---|---|---|---|
|  |  |  |  |
|  |  |  |  |

## SPECIAL EVENTS & MEMORIES
| EVENT | YEAR | EVENT | YEAR |
|---|---|---|---|
|  |  |  |  |
|  |  |  |  |
|  |  |  |  |

# MARCH 13

## BIRTHDAYS
| NAME | YEAR | NAME | YEAR |
|---|---|---|---|
|  |  |  |  |
|  |  |  |  |

## ANNIVERSARIES
| NAME | YEAR | NAME | YEAR |
|---|---|---|---|
|  |  |  |  |
|  |  |  |  |

## SPECIAL EVENTS & MEMORIES
| EVENT | YEAR | EVENT | YEAR |
|---|---|---|---|
|  |  |  |  |
|  |  |  |  |
|  |  |  |  |

## MARCH 14

**BIRTHDAYS**

| NAME | YEAR | NAME | YEAR |
|---|---|---|---|
| | | | |
| | | | |

**ANNIVERSARIES**

| NAME | YEAR | NAME | YEAR |
|---|---|---|---|
| | | | |
| | | | |

**SPECIAL EVENTS & MEMORIES**

| EVENT | YEAR | EVENT | YEAR |
|---|---|---|---|
| | | | |
| | | | |
| | | | |

## MARCH 15

**BIRTHDAYS**

| NAME | YEAR | NAME | YEAR |
|---|---|---|---|
| | | | |
| | | | |

**ANNIVERSARIES**

| NAME | YEAR | NAME | YEAR |
|---|---|---|---|
| | | | |
| | | | |

**SPECIAL EVENTS & MEMORIES**

| EVENT | YEAR | EVENT | YEAR |
|---|---|---|---|
| | | | |
| | | | |
| | | | |

## MARCH 16

**BIRTHDAYS**

| NAME | YEAR | NAME | YEAR |
|---|---|---|---|
| | | | |
| | | | |

**ANNIVERSARIES**

| NAME | YEAR | NAME | YEAR |
|---|---|---|---|
| | | | |
| | | | |

**SPECIAL EVENTS & MEMORIES**

| EVENT | YEAR | EVENT | YEAR |
|---|---|---|---|
| | | | |
| | | | |
| | | | |

# MARCH 17

## BIRTHDAYS
| NAME | YEAR | NAME | YEAR |
|---|---|---|---|
|  |  |  |  |
|  |  |  |  |
|  |  |  |  |

## ANNIVERSARIES
| NAME | YEAR | NAME | YEAR |
|---|---|---|---|
|  |  |  |  |
|  |  |  |  |

## SPECIAL EVENTS & MEMORIES
| EVENT | YEAR | EVENT | YEAR |
|---|---|---|---|
|  |  |  |  |
|  |  |  |  |
|  |  |  |  |
|  |  |  |  |

# MARCH 18

## BIRTHDAYS
| NAME | YEAR | NAME | YEAR |
|---|---|---|---|
|  |  |  |  |
|  |  |  |  |
|  |  |  |  |

## ANNIVERSARIES
| NAME | YEAR | NAME | YEAR |
|---|---|---|---|
|  |  |  |  |
|  |  |  |  |

## SPECIAL EVENTS & MEMORIES
| EVENT | YEAR | EVENT | YEAR |
|---|---|---|---|
|  |  |  |  |
|  |  |  |  |
|  |  |  |  |
|  |  |  |  |

# MARCH 19

## BIRTHDAYS
| NAME | YEAR | NAME | YEAR |
|---|---|---|---|
|  |  |  |  |
|  |  |  |  |
|  |  |  |  |

## ANNIVERSARIES
| NAME | YEAR | NAME | YEAR |
|---|---|---|---|
|  |  |  |  |
|  |  |  |  |

## SPECIAL EVENTS & MEMORIES
| EVENT | YEAR | EVENT | YEAR |
|---|---|---|---|
|  |  |  |  |
|  |  |  |  |
|  |  |  |  |
|  |  |  |  |

## MARCH 20

**BIRTHDAYS**

| NAME | YEAR | NAME | YEAR |
|---|---|---|---|
| | | | |
| | | | |
| | | | |

**ANNIVERSARIES**

| NAME | YEAR | NAME | YEAR |
|---|---|---|---|
| | | | |
| | | | |

**SPECIAL EVENTS & MEMORIES**

| EVENT | YEAR | EVENT | YEAR |
|---|---|---|---|
| | | | |
| | | | |
| | | | |
| | | | |

## MARCH 21

**BIRTHDAYS**

| NAME | YEAR | NAME | YEAR |
|---|---|---|---|
| | | | |
| | | | |
| | | | |

**ANNIVERSARIES**

| NAME | YEAR | NAME | YEAR |
|---|---|---|---|
| | | | |
| | | | |

**SPECIAL EVENTS & MEMORIES**

| EVENT | YEAR | EVENT | YEAR |
|---|---|---|---|
| | | | |
| | | | |
| | | | |
| | | | |

## MARCH 22

**BIRTHDAYS**

| NAME | YEAR | NAME | YEAR |
|---|---|---|---|
| Adeline Campbell | | | |
| | | | |
| | | | |

**ANNIVERSARIES**

| NAME | YEAR | NAME | YEAR |
|---|---|---|---|
| | | | |
| | | | |

**SPECIAL EVENTS & MEMORIES**

| EVENT | YEAR | EVENT | YEAR |
|---|---|---|---|
| | | | |
| | | | |
| | | | |
| | | | |

## MARCH 23

### BIRTHDAYS
| NAME | YEAR | NAME | YEAR |
|---|---|---|---|
| | | | |
| | | | |

### ANNIVERSARIES
| NAME | YEAR | NAME | YEAR |
|---|---|---|---|
| | | | |
| | | | |

### SPECIAL EVENTS & MEMORIES
| EVENT | YEAR | EVENT | YEAR |
|---|---|---|---|
| | | | |
| | | | |
| | | | |

## MARCH 24

### BIRTHDAYS
| NAME | YEAR | NAME | YEAR |
|---|---|---|---|
| Jenny Bryant | | | |
| | | | |

### ANNIVERSARIES
| NAME | YEAR | NAME | YEAR |
|---|---|---|---|
| | | | |
| | | | |

### SPECIAL EVENTS & MEMORIES
| EVENT | YEAR | EVENT | YEAR |
|---|---|---|---|
| | | | |
| | | | |
| | | | |

## MARCH 25

### BIRTHDAYS
| NAME | YEAR | NAME | YEAR |
|---|---|---|---|
| | | | |
| | | | |

### ANNIVERSARIES
| NAME | YEAR | NAME | YEAR |
|---|---|---|---|
| | | | |
| | | | |

### SPECIAL EVENTS & MEMORIES
| EVENT | YEAR | EVENT | YEAR |
|---|---|---|---|
| | | | |
| | | | |
| | | | |

# MARCH 26

**BIRTHDAYS**

| NAME | YEAR | NAME | YEAR |
|------|------|------|------|
|      |      |      |      |
|      |      |      |      |
|      |      |      |      |

**ANNIVERSARIES**

| NAME | YEAR | NAME | YEAR |
|------|------|------|------|
|      |      |      |      |
|      |      |      |      |

**SPECIAL EVENTS & MEMORIES**

| EVENT | YEAR | EVENT | YEAR |
|-------|------|-------|------|
|       |      |       |      |
|       |      |       |      |
|       |      |       |      |
|       |      |       |      |

# MARCH 27

**BIRTHDAYS**

| NAME | YEAR | NAME | YEAR |
|------|------|------|------|
|      |      |      |      |
|      |      |      |      |
|      |      |      |      |

**ANNIVERSARIES**

| NAME | YEAR | NAME | YEAR |
|------|------|------|------|
|      |      |      |      |
|      |      |      |      |

**SPECIAL EVENTS & MEMORIES**

| EVENT | YEAR | EVENT | YEAR |
|-------|------|-------|------|
|       |      |       |      |
|       |      |       |      |
|       |      |       |      |
|       |      |       |      |

# MARCH 28

**BIRTHDAYS**

| NAME | YEAR | NAME | YEAR |
|------|------|------|------|
|      |      |      |      |
|      |      |      |      |
|      |      |      |      |

**ANNIVERSARIES**

| NAME | YEAR | NAME | YEAR |
|------|------|------|------|
|      |      |      |      |
|      |      |      |      |

**SPECIAL EVENTS & MEMORIES**

| EVENT | YEAR | EVENT | YEAR |
|-------|------|-------|------|
|       |      |       |      |
|       |      |       |      |
|       |      |       |      |

## MARCH 29

### BIRTHDAYS
| NAME | YEAR | NAME | YEAR |
|---|---|---|---|
|  |  |  |  |
|  |  |  |  |
|  |  |  |  |

### ANNIVERSARIES
| NAME | YEAR | NAME | YEAR |
|---|---|---|---|
|  |  |  |  |
|  |  |  |  |

### SPECIAL EVENTS & MEMORIES
| EVENT | YEAR | EVENT | YEAR |
|---|---|---|---|
|  |  |  |  |
|  |  |  |  |
|  |  |  |  |
|  |  |  |  |

## MARCH 30

### BIRTHDAYS
| NAME | YEAR | NAME | YEAR |
|---|---|---|---|
|  |  |  |  |
|  |  |  |  |
|  |  |  |  |

### ANNIVERSARIES
| NAME | YEAR | NAME | YEAR |
|---|---|---|---|
|  |  |  |  |
|  |  |  |  |

### SPECIAL EVENTS & MEMORIES
| EVENT | YEAR | EVENT | YEAR |
|---|---|---|---|
|  |  |  |  |
|  |  |  |  |
|  |  |  |  |
|  |  |  |  |

## MARCH 31

### BIRTHDAYS
| NAME | YEAR | NAME | YEAR |
|---|---|---|---|
|  |  |  |  |
|  |  |  |  |
|  |  |  |  |

### ANNIVERSARIES
| NAME | YEAR | NAME | YEAR |
|---|---|---|---|
|  |  |  |  |
|  |  |  |  |

### SPECIAL EVENTS & MEMORIES
| EVENT | YEAR | EVENT | YEAR |
|---|---|---|---|
|  |  |  |  |
|  |  |  |  |
|  |  |  |  |
|  |  |  |  |

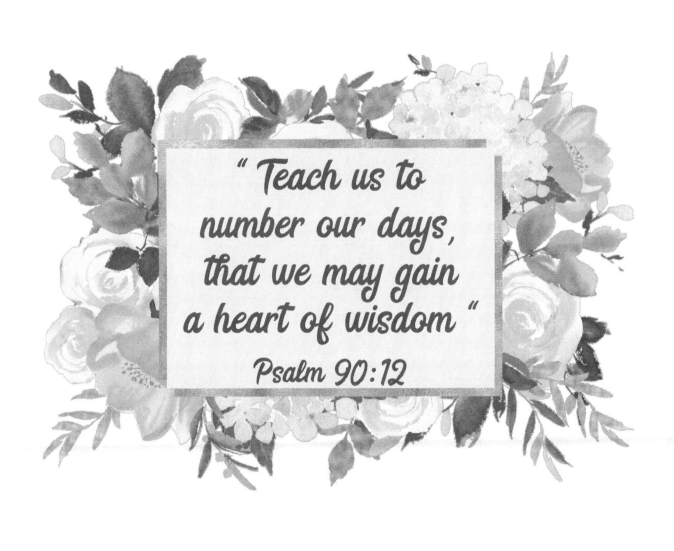

# APRIL 1

## BIRTHDAYS

| NAME | YEAR | NAME | YEAR |
|---|---|---|---|
|  |  |  |  |
|  |  |  |  |
|  |  |  |  |

## ANNIVERSARIES

| NAME | YEAR | NAME | YEAR |
|---|---|---|---|
|  |  |  |  |
|  |  |  |  |

## SPECIAL EVENTS & MEMORIES

| EVENT | YEAR | EVENT | YEAR |
|---|---|---|---|
|  |  |  |  |
|  |  |  |  |
|  |  |  |  |
|  |  |  |  |

## APRIL 2

### BIRTHDAYS

| NAME | YEAR | NAME | YEAR |
|------|------|------|------|
|      |      |      |      |
|      |      |      |      |
|      |      |      |      |

### ANNIVERSARIES

| NAME | YEAR | NAME | YEAR |
|------|------|------|------|
|      |      |      |      |
|      |      |      |      |

### SPECIAL EVENTS & MEMORIES

| EVENT | YEAR | EVENT | YEAR |
|-------|------|-------|------|
|       |      |       |      |
|       |      |       |      |
|       |      |       |      |

## APRIL 3

### BIRTHDAYS

| NAME | YEAR | NAME | YEAR |
|------|------|------|------|
|      |      |      |      |
|      |      |      |      |
|      |      |      |      |

### ANNIVERSARIES

| NAME | YEAR | NAME | YEAR |
|------|------|------|------|
|      |      |      |      |
|      |      |      |      |

### SPECIAL EVENTS & MEMORIES

| EVENT | YEAR | EVENT | YEAR |
|-------|------|-------|------|
|       |      |       |      |
|       |      |       |      |
|       |      |       |      |

## APRIL 4

### BIRTHDAYS

| NAME | YEAR | NAME | YEAR |
|------|------|------|------|
|      |      |      |      |
|      |      |      |      |
|      |      |      |      |

### ANNIVERSARIES

| NAME | YEAR | NAME | YEAR |
|------|------|------|------|
|      |      |      |      |
|      |      |      |      |

### SPECIAL EVENTS & MEMORIES

| EVENT | YEAR | EVENT | YEAR |
|-------|------|-------|------|
|       |      |       |      |
|       |      |       |      |
|       |      |       |      |

## APRIL 5

### BIRTHDAYS

| NAME | YEAR | NAME | YEAR |
|------|------|------|------|
|      |      |      |      |
|      |      |      |      |
|      |      |      |      |

### ANNIVERSARIES

| NAME | YEAR | NAME | YEAR |
|------|------|------|------|
|      |      |      |      |
|      |      |      |      |

### SPECIAL EVENTS & MEMORIES

| EVENT | YEAR | EVENT | YEAR |
|-------|------|-------|------|
|       |      |       |      |
|       |      |       |      |
|       |      |       |      |
|       |      |       |      |

## APRIL 6

### BIRTHDAYS

| NAME | YEAR | NAME | YEAR |
|------|------|------|------|
|      |      |      |      |
|      |      |      |      |
|      |      |      |      |

### ANNIVERSARIES

| NAME | YEAR | NAME | YEAR |
|------|------|------|------|
|      |      |      |      |
|      |      |      |      |

### SPECIAL EVENTS & MEMORIES

| EVENT | YEAR | EVENT | YEAR |
|-------|------|-------|------|
|       |      |       |      |
|       |      |       |      |
|       |      |       |      |
|       |      |       |      |

## APRIL 7

### BIRTHDAYS

| NAME | YEAR | NAME | YEAR |
|------|------|------|------|
|      |      |      |      |
|      |      |      |      |
|      |      |      |      |

### ANNIVERSARIES

| NAME | YEAR | NAME | YEAR |
|------|------|------|------|
|      |      |      |      |
|      |      |      |      |

### SPECIAL EVENTS & MEMORIES

| EVENT | YEAR | EVENT | YEAR |
|-------|------|-------|------|
|       |      |       |      |
|       |      |       |      |
|       |      |       |      |
|       |      |       |      |

## APRIL 8

### BIRTHDAYS

| NAME | YEAR | NAME | YEAR |
|---|---|---|---|
| | | | |
| | | | |
| | | | |

### ANNIVERSARIES

| NAME | YEAR | NAME | YEAR |
|---|---|---|---|
| | | | |
| | | | |

### SPECIAL EVENTS & MEMORIES

| EVENT | YEAR | EVENT | YEAR |
|---|---|---|---|
| | | | |
| | | | |
| | | | |

## APRIL 9

### BIRTHDAYS

| NAME | YEAR | NAME | YEAR |
|---|---|---|---|
| | | | |
| | | | |
| | | | |

### ANNIVERSARIES

| NAME | YEAR | NAME | YEAR |
|---|---|---|---|
| | | | |
| | | | |

### SPECIAL EVENTS & MEMORIES

| EVENT | YEAR | EVENT | YEAR |
|---|---|---|---|
| | | | |
| | | | |
| | | | |

## APRIL 10

### BIRTHDAYS

| NAME | YEAR | NAME | YEAR |
|---|---|---|---|
| | | | |
| | | | |
| | | | |

### ANNIVERSARIES

| NAME | YEAR | NAME | YEAR |
|---|---|---|---|
| | | | |
| | | | |

### SPECIAL EVENTS & MEMORIES

| EVENT | YEAR | EVENT | YEAR |
|---|---|---|---|
| | | | |
| | | | |
| | | | |

# APRIL 11

## BIRTHDAYS
| NAME | YEAR | NAME | YEAR |
|---|---|---|---|
|  |  |  |  |
|  |  |  |  |
|  |  |  |  |

## ANNIVERSARIES
| NAME | YEAR | NAME | YEAR |
|---|---|---|---|
|  |  |  |  |
|  |  |  |  |

## SPECIAL EVENTS & MEMORIES
| EVENT | YEAR | EVENT | YEAR |
|---|---|---|---|
|  |  |  |  |
|  |  |  |  |
|  |  |  |  |
|  |  |  |  |

# APRIL 12

## BIRTHDAYS
| NAME | YEAR | NAME | YEAR |
|---|---|---|---|
|  |  |  |  |
|  |  |  |  |
|  |  |  |  |

## ANNIVERSARIES
| NAME | YEAR | NAME | YEAR |
|---|---|---|---|
|  |  |  |  |
|  |  |  |  |

## SPECIAL EVENTS & MEMORIES
| EVENT | YEAR | EVENT | YEAR |
|---|---|---|---|
|  |  |  |  |
|  |  |  |  |
|  |  |  |  |
|  |  |  |  |

# APRIL 13

## BIRTHDAYS
| NAME | YEAR | NAME | YEAR |
|---|---|---|---|
| Cade Turchick |  |  |  |
|  |  |  |  |
|  |  |  |  |

## ANNIVERSARIES
| NAME | YEAR | NAME | YEAR |
|---|---|---|---|
|  |  |  |  |
|  |  |  |  |

## SPECIAL EVENTS & MEMORIES
| EVENT | YEAR | EVENT | YEAR |
|---|---|---|---|
|  |  |  |  |
|  |  |  |  |
|  |  |  |  |
|  |  |  |  |

## APRIL 14

**BIRTHDAYS**

| NAME | YEAR | NAME | YEAR |
|------|------|------|------|
|      |      |      |      |
|      |      |      |      |

**ANNIVERSARIES**

| NAME | YEAR | NAME | YEAR |
|------|------|------|------|
|      |      |      |      |
|      |      |      |      |

**SPECIAL EVENTS & MEMORIES**

| EVENT | YEAR | EVENT | YEAR |
|-------|------|-------|------|
|       |      |       |      |
|       |      |       |      |
|       |      |       |      |

## APRIL 15

**BIRTHDAYS**

| NAME | YEAR | NAME | YEAR |
|------|------|------|------|
|      |      |      |      |
|      |      |      |      |

**ANNIVERSARIES**

| NAME | YEAR | NAME | YEAR |
|------|------|------|------|
|      |      |      |      |
|      |      |      |      |

**SPECIAL EVENTS & MEMORIES**

| EVENT | YEAR | EVENT | YEAR |
|-------|------|-------|------|
|       |      |       |      |
|       |      |       |      |
|       |      |       |      |

## APRIL 16

**BIRTHDAYS**

| NAME | YEAR | NAME | YEAR |
|------|------|------|------|
|      |      |      |      |
|      |      |      |      |

**ANNIVERSARIES**

| NAME | YEAR | NAME | YEAR |
|------|------|------|------|
|      |      |      |      |
|      |      |      |      |

**SPECIAL EVENTS & MEMORIES**

| EVENT | YEAR | EVENT | YEAR |
|-------|------|-------|------|
|       |      |       |      |
|       |      |       |      |
|       |      |       |      |

## APRIL 17

### BIRTHDAYS
| NAME | YEAR | NAME | YEAR |
|------|------|------|------|
|  |  |  |  |
|  |  |  |  |
|  |  |  |  |

### ANNIVERSARIES
| NAME | YEAR | NAME | YEAR |
|------|------|------|------|
|  |  |  |  |
|  |  |  |  |

### SPECIAL EVENTS & MEMORIES
| EVENT | YEAR | EVENT | YEAR |
|-------|------|-------|------|
|  |  |  |  |
|  |  |  |  |
|  |  |  |  |
|  |  |  |  |

## APRIL 18

### BIRTHDAYS
| NAME | YEAR | NAME | YEAR |
|------|------|------|------|
|  |  |  |  |
|  |  |  |  |
|  |  |  |  |

### ANNIVERSARIES
| NAME | YEAR | NAME | YEAR |
|------|------|------|------|
|  |  |  |  |
|  |  |  |  |

### SPECIAL EVENTS & MEMORIES
| EVENT | YEAR | EVENT | YEAR |
|-------|------|-------|------|
|  |  |  |  |
|  |  |  |  |
|  |  |  |  |
|  |  |  |  |

## APRIL 19

### BIRTHDAYS
| NAME | YEAR | NAME | YEAR |
|------|------|------|------|
|  |  |  |  |
|  |  |  |  |
|  |  |  |  |

### ANNIVERSARIES
| NAME | YEAR | NAME | YEAR |
|------|------|------|------|
|  |  |  |  |
|  |  |  |  |

### SPECIAL EVENTS & MEMORIES
| EVENT | YEAR | EVENT | YEAR |
|-------|------|-------|------|
|  |  |  |  |
|  |  |  |  |
|  |  |  |  |
|  |  |  |  |

## APRIL 20

### BIRTHDAYS
| NAME | YEAR | NAME | YEAR |
|---|---|---|---|
|  |  |  |  |
|  |  |  |  |
|  |  |  |  |

### ANNIVERSARIES
| NAME | YEAR | NAME | YEAR |
|---|---|---|---|
|  |  |  |  |
|  |  |  |  |

### SPECIAL EVENTS & MEMORIES
| EVENT | YEAR | EVENT | YEAR |
|---|---|---|---|
|  |  |  |  |
|  |  |  |  |
|  |  |  |  |
|  |  |  |  |

## APRIL 21

### BIRTHDAYS
| NAME | YEAR | NAME | YEAR |
|---|---|---|---|
|  |  |  |  |
|  |  |  |  |
|  |  |  |  |

### ANNIVERSARIES
| NAME | YEAR | NAME | YEAR |
|---|---|---|---|
|  |  |  |  |
|  |  |  |  |

### SPECIAL EVENTS & MEMORIES
| EVENT | YEAR | EVENT | YEAR |
|---|---|---|---|
|  |  |  |  |
|  |  |  |  |
|  |  |  |  |
|  |  |  |  |

## APRIL 22

### BIRTHDAYS
| NAME | YEAR | NAME | YEAR |
|---|---|---|---|
|  |  |  |  |
|  |  |  |  |
|  |  |  |  |

### ANNIVERSARIES
| NAME | YEAR | NAME | YEAR |
|---|---|---|---|
|  |  |  |  |
|  |  |  |  |

### SPECIAL EVENTS & MEMORIES
| EVENT | YEAR | EVENT | YEAR |
|---|---|---|---|
|  |  |  |  |
|  |  |  |  |
|  |  |  |  |
|  |  |  |  |

## APRIL 23

### BIRTHDAYS

| NAME | YEAR | NAME | YEAR |
|---|---|---|---|
| | | | |
| | | | |
| | | | |

### ANNIVERSARIES

| NAME | YEAR | NAME | YEAR |
|---|---|---|---|
| | | | |
| | | | |

### SPECIAL EVENTS & MEMORIES

| EVENT | YEAR | EVENT | YEAR |
|---|---|---|---|
| | | | |
| | | | |
| | | | |
| | | | |

## APRIL 24

### BIRTHDAYS

| NAME | YEAR | NAME | YEAR |
|---|---|---|---|
| | | | |
| | | | |
| | | | |

### ANNIVERSARIES

| NAME | YEAR | NAME | YEAR |
|---|---|---|---|
| | | | |
| | | | |

### SPECIAL EVENTS & MEMORIES

| EVENT | YEAR | EVENT | YEAR |
|---|---|---|---|
| | | | |
| | | | |
| | | | |
| | | | |

## APRIL 25

### BIRTHDAYS

| NAME | YEAR | NAME | YEAR |
|---|---|---|---|
| | | | |
| | | | |
| | | | |

### ANNIVERSARIES

| NAME | YEAR | NAME | YEAR |
|---|---|---|---|
| | | | |
| | | | |

### SPECIAL EVENTS & MEMORIES

| EVENT | YEAR | EVENT | YEAR |
|---|---|---|---|
| | | | |
| | | | |
| | | | |
| | | | |

## APRIL 26

### BIRTHDAYS

| NAME | YEAR | NAME | YEAR |
|------|------|------|------|
|  |  |  |  |
|  |  |  |  |

### ANNIVERSARIES

| NAME | YEAR | NAME | YEAR |
|------|------|------|------|
|  |  |  |  |
|  |  |  |  |

### SPECIAL EVENTS & MEMORIES

| EVENT | YEAR | EVENT | YEAR |
|-------|------|-------|------|
|  |  |  |  |
|  |  |  |  |
|  |  |  |  |

## APRIL 27

### BIRTHDAYS

| NAME | YEAR | NAME | YEAR |
|------|------|------|------|
|  |  |  |  |
|  |  |  |  |
|  |  |  |  |

### ANNIVERSARIES

| NAME | YEAR | NAME | YEAR |
|------|------|------|------|
|  |  |  |  |
|  |  |  |  |

### SPECIAL EVENTS & MEMORIES

| EVENT | YEAR | EVENT | YEAR |
|-------|------|-------|------|
|  |  |  |  |
|  |  |  |  |
|  |  |  |  |

## APRIL 28

### BIRTHDAYS

| NAME | YEAR | NAME | YEAR |
|------|------|------|------|
| Beth Ann ~~Costello~~ Olszeski |  |  |  |
|  |  |  |  |
|  |  |  |  |

### ANNIVERSARIES

| NAME | YEAR | NAME | YEAR |
|------|------|------|------|
|  |  |  |  |
|  |  |  |  |

### SPECIAL EVENTS & MEMORIES

| EVENT | YEAR | EVENT | YEAR |
|-------|------|-------|------|
|  |  |  |  |
|  |  |  |  |
|  |  |  |  |

## APRIL 29

### BIRTHDAYS

| NAME | YEAR | NAME | YEAR |
|---|---|---|---|
|  |  |  |  |
|  |  |  |  |
|  |  |  |  |

### ANNIVERSARIES

| NAME | YEAR | NAME | YEAR |
|---|---|---|---|
|  |  |  |  |
|  |  |  |  |

### SPECIAL EVENTS & MEMORIES

| EVENT | YEAR | EVENT | YEAR |
|---|---|---|---|
|  |  |  |  |
|  |  |  |  |
|  |  |  |  |
|  |  |  |  |

## APRIL 30

### BIRTHDAYS

| NAME | YEAR | NAME | YEAR |
|---|---|---|---|
|  |  |  |  |
|  |  |  |  |
|  |  |  |  |

### ANNIVERSARIES

| NAME | YEAR | NAME | YEAR |
|---|---|---|---|
|  |  |  |  |
|  |  |  |  |

### SPECIAL EVENTS & MEMORIES

| EVENT | YEAR | EVENT | YEAR |
|---|---|---|---|
|  |  |  |  |
|  |  |  |  |
|  |  |  |  |
|  |  |  |  |

## NOTES:

## MAY 1

### BIRTHDAYS
| NAME | YEAR | NAME | YEAR |
|------|------|------|------|
|      |      |      |      |
|      |      |      |      |
|      |      |      |      |

### ANNIVERSARIES
| NAME | YEAR | NAME | YEAR |
|------|------|------|------|
|      |      |      |      |
|      |      |      |      |

### SPECIAL EVENTS & MEMORIES
| EVENT | YEAR | EVENT | YEAR |
|-------|------|-------|------|
|       |      |       |      |
|       |      |       |      |
|       |      |       |      |
|       |      |       |      |

# MAY 2

## BIRTHDAYS
| NAME | YEAR | NAME | YEAR |
|---|---|---|---|
| | | | |
| | | | |
| | | | |

## ANNIVERSARIES
| NAME | YEAR | NAME | YEAR |
|---|---|---|---|
| | | | |
| | | | |

## SPECIAL EVENTS & MEMORIES
| EVENT | YEAR | EVENT | YEAR |
|---|---|---|---|
| | | | |
| | | | |
| | | | |
| | | | |

# MAY 3

## BIRTHDAYS
| NAME | YEAR | NAME | YEAR |
|---|---|---|---|
| | | | |
| | | | |
| | | | |

## ANNIVERSARIES
| NAME | YEAR | NAME | YEAR |
|---|---|---|---|
| | | | |
| | | | |

## SPECIAL EVENTS & MEMORIES
| EVENT | YEAR | EVENT | YEAR |
|---|---|---|---|
| | | | |
| | | | |
| | | | |
| | | | |

# MAY 4

## BIRTHDAYS
| NAME | YEAR | NAME | YEAR |
|---|---|---|---|
| | | | |
| | | | |
| | | | |

## ANNIVERSARIES
| NAME | YEAR | NAME | YEAR |
|---|---|---|---|
| | | | |
| | | | |

## SPECIAL EVENTS & MEMORIES
| EVENT | YEAR | EVENT | YEAR |
|---|---|---|---|
| | | | |
| | | | |
| | | | |
| | | | |

## MAY 5

### BIRTHDAYS
| NAME | YEAR | NAME | YEAR |
|---|---|---|---|
|  |  |  |  |
|  |  |  |  |
|  |  |  |  |

### ANNIVERSARIES
| NAME | YEAR | NAME | YEAR |
|---|---|---|---|
|  |  |  |  |
|  |  |  |  |

### SPECIAL EVENTS & MEMORIES
| EVENT | YEAR | EVENT | YEAR |
|---|---|---|---|
|  |  |  |  |
|  |  |  |  |
|  |  |  |  |
|  |  |  |  |

## MAY 6

### BIRTHDAYS
| NAME | YEAR | NAME | YEAR |
|---|---|---|---|
|  |  |  |  |
|  |  |  |  |
|  |  |  |  |

### ANNIVERSARIES
| NAME | YEAR | NAME | YEAR |
|---|---|---|---|
|  |  |  |  |
|  |  |  |  |

### SPECIAL EVENTS & MEMORIES
| EVENT | YEAR | EVENT | YEAR |
|---|---|---|---|
|  |  |  |  |
|  |  |  |  |
|  |  |  |  |
|  |  |  |  |

## MAY 7

### BIRTHDAYS
| NAME | YEAR | NAME | YEAR |
|---|---|---|---|
|  |  |  |  |
|  |  |  |  |
|  |  |  |  |

### ANNIVERSARIES
| NAME | YEAR | NAME | YEAR |
|---|---|---|---|
|  |  |  |  |
|  |  |  |  |

### SPECIAL EVENTS & MEMORIES
| EVENT | YEAR | EVENT | YEAR |
|---|---|---|---|
|  |  |  |  |
|  |  |  |  |
|  |  |  |  |
|  |  |  |  |

# MAY 8

### BIRTHDAYS
| NAME | YEAR | NAME | YEAR |
|---|---|---|---|
|  |  |  |  |
|  |  |  |  |

### ANNIVERSARIES
| NAME | YEAR | NAME | YEAR |
|---|---|---|---|
|  |  |  |  |
|  |  |  |  |

### SPECIAL EVENTS & MEMORIES
| EVENT | YEAR | EVENT | YEAR |
|---|---|---|---|
|  |  |  |  |
|  |  |  |  |
|  |  |  |  |

# MAY 9

### BIRTHDAYS
| NAME | YEAR | NAME | YEAR |
|---|---|---|---|
|  |  |  |  |
|  |  |  |  |
|  |  |  |  |

### ANNIVERSARIES
| NAME | YEAR | NAME | YEAR |
|---|---|---|---|
|  |  |  |  |
|  |  |  |  |

### SPECIAL EVENTS & MEMORIES
| EVENT | YEAR | EVENT | YEAR |
|---|---|---|---|
|  |  |  |  |
|  |  |  |  |
|  |  |  |  |

# MAY 10

### BIRTHDAYS
| NAME | YEAR | NAME | YEAR |
|---|---|---|---|
|  |  |  |  |
|  |  |  |  |
|  |  |  |  |

### ANNIVERSARIES
| NAME | YEAR | NAME | YEAR |
|---|---|---|---|
|  |  |  |  |
|  |  |  |  |

### SPECIAL EVENTS & MEMORIES
| EVENT | YEAR | EVENT | YEAR |
|---|---|---|---|
|  |  |  |  |
|  |  |  |  |
|  |  |  |  |

## MAY 11

### BIRTHDAYS
| NAME | YEAR | NAME | YEAR |
|---|---|---|---|
| | | | |
| | | | |
| | | | |

### ANNIVERSARIES
| NAME | YEAR | NAME | YEAR |
|---|---|---|---|
| | | | |
| | | | |

### SPECIAL EVENTS & MEMORIES
| EVENT | YEAR | EVENT | YEAR |
|---|---|---|---|
| | | | |
| | | | |
| | | | |
| | | | |

## MAY 12

### BIRTHDAYS
| NAME | YEAR | NAME | YEAR |
|---|---|---|---|
| | | | |
| | | | |
| | | | |

### ANNIVERSARIES
| NAME | YEAR | NAME | YEAR |
|---|---|---|---|
| | | | |
| | | | |

### SPECIAL EVENTS & MEMORIES
| EVENT | YEAR | EVENT | YEAR |
|---|---|---|---|
| | | | |
| | | | |
| | | | |
| | | | |

## MAY 13

### BIRTHDAYS
| NAME | YEAR | NAME | YEAR |
|---|---|---|---|
| Tina Stone | 1975 | | |
| | | | |
| | | | |

### ANNIVERSARIES
| NAME | YEAR | NAME | YEAR |
|---|---|---|---|
| | | | |
| | | | |

### SPECIAL EVENTS & MEMORIES
| EVENT | YEAR | EVENT | YEAR |
|---|---|---|---|
| | | | |
| | | | |
| | | | |
| | | | |

# MAY 14

## BIRTHDAYS
| NAME | YEAR | NAME | YEAR |
|---|---|---|---|
| | | | |
| | | | |

## ANNIVERSARIES
| NAME | YEAR | NAME | YEAR |
|---|---|---|---|
| | | | |
| | | | |

## SPECIAL EVENTS & MEMORIES
| EVENT | YEAR | EVENT | YEAR |
|---|---|---|---|
| | | | |
| | | | |
| | | | |

# MAY 15

## BIRTHDAYS
| NAME | YEAR | NAME | YEAR |
|---|---|---|---|
| | | | |
| | | | |
| | | | |

## ANNIVERSARIES
| NAME | YEAR | NAME | YEAR |
|---|---|---|---|
| | | | |
| | | | |

## SPECIAL EVENTS & MEMORIES
| EVENT | YEAR | EVENT | YEAR |
|---|---|---|---|
| | | | |
| | | | |
| | | | |

# MAY 16

## BIRTHDAYS
| NAME | YEAR | NAME | YEAR |
|---|---|---|---|
| | | | |
| | | | |
| | | | |

## ANNIVERSARIES
| NAME | YEAR | NAME | YEAR |
|---|---|---|---|
| | | | |
| | | | |

## SPECIAL EVENTS & MEMORIES
| EVENT | YEAR | EVENT | YEAR |
|---|---|---|---|
| | | | |
| | | | |
| | | | |

## MAY 17

**BIRTHDAYS**

| NAME | YEAR | NAME | YEAR |
|---|---|---|---|
| | | | |
| | | | |
| | | | |

**ANNIVERSARIES**

| NAME | YEAR | NAME | YEAR |
|---|---|---|---|
| | | | |
| | | | |

**SPECIAL EVENTS & MEMORIES**

| EVENT | YEAR | EVENT | YEAR |
|---|---|---|---|
| | | | |
| | | | |
| | | | |
| | | | |

## MAY 18

**BIRTHDAYS**

| NAME | YEAR | NAME | YEAR |
|---|---|---|---|
| | | | |
| | | | |
| | | | |

**ANNIVERSARIES**

| NAME | YEAR | NAME | YEAR |
|---|---|---|---|
| | | | |
| | | | |

**SPECIAL EVENTS & MEMORIES**

| EVENT | YEAR | EVENT | YEAR |
|---|---|---|---|
| | | | |
| | | | |
| | | | |
| | | | |

## MAY 19

**BIRTHDAYS**

| NAME | YEAR | NAME | YEAR |
|---|---|---|---|
| | | | |
| | | | |
| | | | |

**ANNIVERSARIES**

| NAME | YEAR | NAME | YEAR |
|---|---|---|---|
| | | | |
| | | | |

**SPECIAL EVENTS & MEMORIES**

| EVENT | YEAR | EVENT | YEAR |
|---|---|---|---|
| | | | |
| | | | |
| | | | |
| | | | |

## MAY 20

### BIRTHDAYS
| NAME | YEAR | NAME | YEAR |
|---|---|---|---|
|  |  |  |  |
|  |  |  |  |
|  |  |  |  |

### ANNIVERSARIES
| NAME | YEAR | NAME | YEAR |
|---|---|---|---|
|  |  |  |  |
|  |  |  |  |

### SPECIAL EVENTS & MEMORIES
| EVENT | YEAR | EVENT | YEAR |
|---|---|---|---|
|  |  |  |  |
|  |  |  |  |
|  |  |  |  |

## MAY 21

### BIRTHDAYS
| NAME | YEAR | NAME | YEAR |
|---|---|---|---|
|  |  |  |  |
|  |  |  |  |
|  |  |  |  |

### ANNIVERSARIES
| NAME | YEAR | NAME | YEAR |
|---|---|---|---|
|  |  |  |  |
|  |  |  |  |

### SPECIAL EVENTS & MEMORIES
| EVENT | YEAR | EVENT | YEAR |
|---|---|---|---|
|  |  |  |  |
|  |  |  |  |
|  |  |  |  |

## MAY 22

### BIRTHDAYS
| NAME | YEAR | NAME | YEAR |
|---|---|---|---|
|  |  |  |  |
|  |  |  |  |
|  |  |  |  |

### ANNIVERSARIES
| NAME | YEAR | NAME | YEAR |
|---|---|---|---|
| Our Anniversary ♥ | 2021 |  |  |
|  |  |  |  |

### SPECIAL EVENTS & MEMORIES
| EVENT | YEAR | EVENT | YEAR |
|---|---|---|---|
|  |  |  |  |
|  |  |  |  |
|  |  |  |  |

## MAY 23

### BIRTHDAYS

| NAME | YEAR | NAME | YEAR |
|---|---|---|---|
| | | | |
| | | | |
| | | | |

### ANNIVERSARIES

| NAME | YEAR | NAME | YEAR |
|---|---|---|---|
| | | | |
| | | | |

### SPECIAL EVENTS & MEMORIES

| EVENT | YEAR | EVENT | YEAR |
|---|---|---|---|
| | | | |
| | | | |
| | | | |
| | | | |

## MAY 24

### BIRTHDAYS

| NAME | YEAR | NAME | YEAR |
|---|---|---|---|
| | | | |
| | | | |
| | | | |

### ANNIVERSARIES

| NAME | YEAR | NAME | YEAR |
|---|---|---|---|
| | | | |
| | | | |

### SPECIAL EVENTS & MEMORIES

| EVENT | YEAR | EVENT | YEAR |
|---|---|---|---|
| | | | |
| | | | |
| | | | |
| | | | |

## MAY 25

### BIRTHDAYS

| NAME | YEAR | NAME | YEAR |
|---|---|---|---|
| | | | |
| | | | |
| | | | |

### ANNIVERSARIES

| NAME | YEAR | NAME | YEAR |
|---|---|---|---|
| | | | |
| | | | |

### SPECIAL EVENTS & MEMORIES

| EVENT | YEAR | EVENT | YEAR |
|---|---|---|---|
| | | | |
| | | | |
| | | | |
| | | | |

## MAY 26

**BIRTHDAYS**

| NAME | YEAR | NAME | YEAR |
|---|---|---|---|
| | | | |
| | | | |

**ANNIVERSARIES**

| NAME | YEAR | NAME | YEAR |
|---|---|---|---|
| | | | |

**SPECIAL EVENTS & MEMORIES**

| EVENT | YEAR | EVENT | YEAR |
|---|---|---|---|
| | | | |
| | | | |
| | | | |

## MAY 27

**BIRTHDAYS**

| NAME | YEAR | NAME | YEAR |
|---|---|---|---|
| | | | |
| | | | |

**ANNIVERSARIES**

| NAME | YEAR | NAME | YEAR |
|---|---|---|---|
| | | | |
| | | | |

**SPECIAL EVENTS & MEMORIES**

| EVENT | YEAR | EVENT | YEAR |
|---|---|---|---|
| | | | |
| | | | |
| | | | |

## MAY 28

**BIRTHDAYS**

| NAME | YEAR | NAME | YEAR |
|---|---|---|---|
| | | | |
| | | | |

**ANNIVERSARIES**

| NAME | YEAR | NAME | YEAR |
|---|---|---|---|
| | | | |
| | | | |

**SPECIAL EVENTS & MEMORIES**

| EVENT | YEAR | EVENT | YEAR |
|---|---|---|---|
| | | | |
| | | | |
| | | | |

# MAY 29

## BIRTHDAYS
| NAME | YEAR | NAME | YEAR |
|---|---|---|---|
|  |  |  |  |
|  |  |  |  |
|  |  |  |  |

## ANNIVERSARIES
| NAME | YEAR | NAME | YEAR |
|---|---|---|---|
|  |  |  |  |
|  |  |  |  |

## SPECIAL EVENTS & MEMORIES
| EVENT | YEAR | EVENT | YEAR |
|---|---|---|---|
|  |  |  |  |
|  |  |  |  |
|  |  |  |  |
|  |  |  |  |

# MAY 30

## BIRTHDAYS
| NAME | YEAR | NAME | YEAR |
|---|---|---|---|
|  |  |  |  |
|  |  |  |  |
|  |  |  |  |

## ANNIVERSARIES
| NAME | YEAR | NAME | YEAR |
|---|---|---|---|
|  |  |  |  |
|  |  |  |  |

## SPECIAL EVENTS & MEMORIES
| EVENT | YEAR | EVENT | YEAR |
|---|---|---|---|
|  |  |  |  |
|  |  |  |  |
|  |  |  |  |
|  |  |  |  |

# MAY 31

## BIRTHDAYS
| NAME | YEAR | NAME | YEAR |
|---|---|---|---|
|  |  |  |  |
|  |  |  |  |
|  |  |  |  |

## ANNIVERSARIES
| NAME | YEAR | NAME | YEAR |
|---|---|---|---|
|  |  |  |  |
|  |  |  |  |

## SPECIAL EVENTS & MEMORIES
| EVENT | YEAR | EVENT | YEAR |
|---|---|---|---|
|  |  |  |  |
|  |  |  |  |
|  |  |  |  |
|  |  |  |  |

# JUNE 1

### BIRTHDAYS

| NAME | YEAR | NAME | YEAR |
|---|---|---|---|
| | | | |
| | | | |
| | | | |

### ANNIVERSARIES

| NAME | YEAR | NAME | YEAR |
|---|---|---|---|
| | | | |
| | | | |

### SPECIAL EVENTS & MEMORIES

| EVENT | YEAR | EVENT | YEAR |
|---|---|---|---|
| | | | |
| | | | |
| | | | |
| | | | |

## JUNE 2

### BIRTHDAYS
| NAME | YEAR | NAME | YEAR |
|------|------|------|------|
|      |      |      |      |
|      |      |      |      |
|      |      |      |      |

### ANNIVERSARIES
| NAME | YEAR | NAME | YEAR |
|------|------|------|------|
|      |      |      |      |
|      |      |      |      |

### SPECIAL EVENTS & MEMORIES
| EVENT | YEAR | EVENT | YEAR |
|-------|------|-------|------|
|       |      |       |      |
|       |      |       |      |
|       |      |       |      |
|       |      |       |      |

## JUNE 3

### BIRTHDAYS
| NAME | YEAR | NAME | YEAR |
|------|------|------|------|
|      |      |      |      |
|      |      |      |      |
|      |      |      |      |

### ANNIVERSARIES
| NAME | YEAR | NAME | YEAR |
|------|------|------|------|
|      |      |      |      |
|      |      |      |      |

### SPECIAL EVENTS & MEMORIES
| EVENT | YEAR | EVENT | YEAR |
|-------|------|-------|------|
|       |      |       |      |
|       |      |       |      |
|       |      |       |      |
|       |      |       |      |

## JUNE 4

### BIRTHDAYS
| NAME | YEAR | NAME | YEAR |
|------|------|------|------|
|      |      |      |      |
|      |      |      |      |
|      |      |      |      |

### ANNIVERSARIES
| NAME | YEAR | NAME | YEAR |
|------|------|------|------|
|      |      |      |      |
|      |      |      |      |

### SPECIAL EVENTS & MEMORIES
| EVENT | YEAR | EVENT | YEAR |
|-------|------|-------|------|
|       |      |       |      |
|       |      |       |      |
|       |      |       |      |
|       |      |       |      |

## JUNE 5

### BIRTHDAYS
| NAME | YEAR | NAME | YEAR |
|---|---|---|---|
|  |  |  |  |
|  |  |  |  |
|  |  |  |  |

### ANNIVERSARIES
| NAME | YEAR | NAME | YEAR |
|---|---|---|---|
|  |  |  |  |
|  |  |  |  |

### SPECIAL EVENTS & MEMORIES
| EVENT | YEAR | EVENT | YEAR |
|---|---|---|---|
|  |  |  |  |
|  |  |  |  |
|  |  |  |  |
|  |  |  |  |

## JUNE 6

### BIRTHDAYS
| NAME | YEAR | NAME | YEAR |
|---|---|---|---|
|  |  |  |  |
|  |  |  |  |
|  |  |  |  |

### ANNIVERSARIES
| NAME | YEAR | NAME | YEAR |
|---|---|---|---|
|  |  |  |  |
|  |  |  |  |

### SPECIAL EVENTS & MEMORIES
| EVENT | YEAR | EVENT | YEAR |
|---|---|---|---|
|  |  |  |  |
|  |  |  |  |
|  |  |  |  |
|  |  |  |  |

## JUNE 7

### BIRTHDAYS
| NAME | YEAR | NAME | YEAR |
|---|---|---|---|
|  |  |  |  |
|  |  |  |  |
|  |  |  |  |

### ANNIVERSARIES
| NAME | YEAR | NAME | YEAR |
|---|---|---|---|
|  |  |  |  |
|  |  |  |  |

### SPECIAL EVENTS & MEMORIES
| EVENT | YEAR | EVENT | YEAR |
|---|---|---|---|
|  |  |  |  |
|  |  |  |  |
|  |  |  |  |
|  |  |  |  |

## JUNE 8

### BIRTHDAYS
| NAME | YEAR | NAME | YEAR |
|---|---|---|---|
|  |  |  |  |
|  |  |  |  |
|  |  |  |  |

### ANNIVERSARIES
| NAME | YEAR | NAME | YEAR |
|---|---|---|---|
|  |  |  |  |
|  |  |  |  |

### SPECIAL EVENTS & MEMORIES
| EVENT | YEAR | EVENT | YEAR |
|---|---|---|---|
|  |  |  |  |
|  |  |  |  |
|  |  |  |  |

## JUNE 9

### BIRTHDAYS
| NAME | YEAR | NAME | YEAR |
|---|---|---|---|
|  |  |  |  |
|  |  |  |  |
|  |  |  |  |

### ANNIVERSARIES
| NAME | YEAR | NAME | YEAR |
|---|---|---|---|
|  |  |  |  |
|  |  |  |  |

### SPECIAL EVENTS & MEMORIES
| EVENT | YEAR | EVENT | YEAR |
|---|---|---|---|
|  |  |  |  |
|  |  |  |  |
|  |  |  |  |

## JUNE 10

### BIRTHDAYS
| NAME | YEAR | NAME | YEAR |
|---|---|---|---|
|  |  |  |  |
|  |  |  |  |
|  |  |  |  |

### ANNIVERSARIES
| NAME | YEAR | NAME | YEAR |
|---|---|---|---|
|  |  |  |  |
|  |  |  |  |

### SPECIAL EVENTS & MEMORIES
| EVENT | YEAR | EVENT | YEAR |
|---|---|---|---|
|  |  |  |  |
|  |  |  |  |
|  |  |  |  |

## JUNE 11

**BIRTHDAYS**

| NAME | YEAR | NAME | YEAR |
|---|---|---|---|
| | | | |
| | | | |
| | | | |

**ANNIVERSARIES**

| NAME | YEAR | NAME | YEAR |
|---|---|---|---|
| | | | |
| | | | |

**SPECIAL EVENTS & MEMORIES**

| EVENT | YEAR | EVENT | YEAR |
|---|---|---|---|
| | | | |
| | | | |
| | | | |
| | | | |

## JUNE 12

**BIRTHDAYS**

| NAME | YEAR | NAME | YEAR |
|---|---|---|---|
| | | | |
| | | | |
| | | | |

**ANNIVERSARIES**

| NAME | YEAR | NAME | YEAR |
|---|---|---|---|
| | | | |
| | | | |

**SPECIAL EVENTS & MEMORIES**

| EVENT | YEAR | EVENT | YEAR |
|---|---|---|---|
| | | | |
| | | | |
| | | | |
| | | | |

## JUNE 13

**BIRTHDAYS**

| NAME | YEAR | NAME | YEAR |
|---|---|---|---|
| | | | |
| | | | |
| | | | |

**ANNIVERSARIES**

| NAME | YEAR | NAME | YEAR |
|---|---|---|---|
| | | | |
| | | | |

**SPECIAL EVENTS & MEMORIES**

| EVENT | YEAR | EVENT | YEAR |
|---|---|---|---|
| | | | |
| | | | |
| | | | |
| | | | |

## JUNE 14

**BIRTHDAYS**

| NAME | YEAR | NAME | YEAR |
|---|---|---|---|
|  |  |  |  |
|  |  |  |  |
|  |  |  |  |

**ANNIVERSARIES**

| NAME | YEAR | NAME | YEAR |
|---|---|---|---|
|  |  |  |  |
|  |  |  |  |

**SPECIAL EVENTS & MEMORIES**

| EVENT | YEAR | EVENT | YEAR |
|---|---|---|---|
|  |  |  |  |
|  |  |  |  |
|  |  |  |  |

## JUNE 15

**BIRTHDAYS**

| NAME | YEAR | NAME | YEAR |
|---|---|---|---|
|  |  |  |  |
|  |  |  |  |
|  |  |  |  |

**ANNIVERSARIES**

| NAME | YEAR | NAME | YEAR |
|---|---|---|---|
|  |  |  |  |
|  |  |  |  |

**SPECIAL EVENTS & MEMORIES**

| EVENT | YEAR | EVENT | YEAR |
|---|---|---|---|
|  |  |  |  |
|  |  |  |  |
|  |  |  |  |

## JUNE 16

**BIRTHDAYS**

| NAME | YEAR | NAME | YEAR |
|---|---|---|---|
|  |  |  |  |
|  |  |  |  |
|  |  |  |  |

**ANNIVERSARIES**

| NAME | YEAR | NAME | YEAR |
|---|---|---|---|
|  |  |  |  |
|  |  |  |  |

**SPECIAL EVENTS & MEMORIES**

| EVENT | YEAR | EVENT | YEAR |
|---|---|---|---|
|  |  |  |  |
|  |  |  |  |
|  |  |  |  |

## JUNE 17

### BIRTHDAYS
| NAME | YEAR | NAME | YEAR |
|---|---|---|---|
| | | | |
| | | | |
| | | | |

### ANNIVERSARIES
| NAME | YEAR | NAME | YEAR |
|---|---|---|---|
| | | | |
| | | | |

### SPECIAL EVENTS & MEMORIES
| EVENT | YEAR | EVENT | YEAR |
|---|---|---|---|
| | | | |
| | | | |
| | | | |
| | | | |

## JUNE 18

### BIRTHDAYS
| NAME | YEAR | NAME | YEAR |
|---|---|---|---|
| | | | |
| | | | |
| | | | |

### ANNIVERSARIES
| NAME | YEAR | NAME | YEAR |
|---|---|---|---|
| | | | |
| | | | |

### SPECIAL EVENTS & MEMORIES
| EVENT | YEAR | EVENT | YEAR |
|---|---|---|---|
| | | | |
| | | | |
| | | | |
| | | | |

## JUNE 19

### BIRTHDAYS
| NAME | YEAR | NAME | YEAR |
|---|---|---|---|
| | | | |
| | | | |
| | | | |

### ANNIVERSARIES
| NAME | YEAR | NAME | YEAR |
|---|---|---|---|
| | | | |
| | | | |

### SPECIAL EVENTS & MEMORIES
| EVENT | YEAR | EVENT | YEAR |
|---|---|---|---|
| | | | |
| | | | |
| | | | |
| | | | |

## JUNE 20

### BIRTHDAYS

| NAME | YEAR | NAME | YEAR |
|---|---|---|---|
| | | | |
| | | | |
| | | | |

### ANNIVERSARIES

| NAME | YEAR | NAME | YEAR |
|---|---|---|---|
| | | | |
| | | | |

### SPECIAL EVENTS & MEMORIES

| EVENT | YEAR | EVENT | YEAR |
|---|---|---|---|
| | | | |
| | | | |
| | | | |

## JUNE 21

### BIRTHDAYS

| NAME | YEAR | NAME | YEAR |
|---|---|---|---|
| | | | |
| | | | |
| | | | |

### ANNIVERSARIES

| NAME | YEAR | NAME | YEAR |
|---|---|---|---|
| | | | |
| | | | |

### SPECIAL EVENTS & MEMORIES

| EVENT | YEAR | EVENT | YEAR |
|---|---|---|---|
| | | | |
| | | | |
| | | | |

## JUNE 22

### BIRTHDAYS

| NAME | YEAR | NAME | YEAR |
|---|---|---|---|
| | | | |
| | | | |
| | | | |

### ANNIVERSARIES

| NAME | YEAR | NAME | YEAR |
|---|---|---|---|
| | | | |
| | | | |

### SPECIAL EVENTS & MEMORIES

| EVENT | YEAR | EVENT | YEAR |
|---|---|---|---|
| | | | |
| | | | |
| | | | |

## JUNE 23

### BIRTHDAYS
| NAME | YEAR | NAME | YEAR |
|------|------|------|------|
|      |      |      |      |
|      |      |      |      |
|      |      |      |      |

### ANNIVERSARIES
| NAME | YEAR | NAME | YEAR |
|------|------|------|------|
|      |      |      |      |
|      |      |      |      |

### SPECIAL EVENTS & MEMORIES
| EVENT | YEAR | EVENT | YEAR |
|-------|------|-------|------|
|       |      |       |      |
|       |      |       |      |
|       |      |       |      |
|       |      |       |      |

## JUNE 24

### BIRTHDAYS
| NAME | YEAR | NAME | YEAR |
|------|------|------|------|
|      |      |      |      |
|      |      |      |      |
|      |      |      |      |

### ANNIVERSARIES
| NAME | YEAR | NAME | YEAR |
|------|------|------|------|
|      |      |      |      |
|      |      |      |      |

### SPECIAL EVENTS & MEMORIES
| EVENT | YEAR | EVENT | YEAR |
|-------|------|-------|------|
|       |      |       |      |
|       |      |       |      |
|       |      |       |      |
|       |      |       |      |

## JUNE 25

### BIRTHDAYS
| NAME | YEAR | NAME | YEAR |
|------|------|------|------|
|      |      |      |      |
|      |      |      |      |
|      |      |      |      |

### ANNIVERSARIES
| NAME | YEAR | NAME | YEAR |
|------|------|------|------|
|      |      |      |      |
|      |      |      |      |

### SPECIAL EVENTS & MEMORIES
| EVENT | YEAR | EVENT | YEAR |
|-------|------|-------|------|
|       |      |       |      |
|       |      |       |      |
|       |      |       |      |
|       |      |       |      |

## JUNE 26

### BIRTHDAYS
| NAME | YEAR | NAME | YEAR |
|---|---|---|---|
|  |  |  |  |
|  |  |  |  |
|  |  |  |  |

### ANNIVERSARIES
| NAME | YEAR | NAME | YEAR |
|---|---|---|---|
|  |  |  |  |
|  |  |  |  |

### SPECIAL EVENTS & MEMORIES
| EVENT | YEAR | EVENT | YEAR |
|---|---|---|---|
|  |  |  |  |
|  |  |  |  |
|  |  |  |  |
|  |  |  |  |

## JUNE 27

### BIRTHDAYS
| NAME | YEAR | NAME | YEAR |
|---|---|---|---|
|  |  |  |  |
|  |  |  |  |
|  |  |  |  |

### ANNIVERSARIES
| NAME | YEAR | NAME | YEAR |
|---|---|---|---|
|  |  |  |  |
|  |  |  |  |

### SPECIAL EVENTS & MEMORIES
| EVENT | YEAR | EVENT | YEAR |
|---|---|---|---|
|  |  |  |  |
|  |  |  |  |
|  |  |  |  |
|  |  |  |  |

## JUNE 28

### BIRTHDAYS
| NAME | YEAR | NAME | YEAR |
|---|---|---|---|
| Rick Harris | 1963 |  |  |
|  |  |  |  |
|  |  |  |  |

### ANNIVERSARIES
| NAME | YEAR | NAME | YEAR |
|---|---|---|---|
|  |  |  |  |
|  |  |  |  |

### SPECIAL EVENTS & MEMORIES
| EVENT | YEAR | EVENT | YEAR |
|---|---|---|---|
|  |  |  |  |
|  |  |  |  |
|  |  |  |  |
|  |  |  |  |

## JUNE 29

### BIRTHDAYS
| NAME | YEAR | NAME | YEAR |
|------|------|------|------|
|      |      |      |      |
|      |      |      |      |
|      |      |      |      |

### ANNIVERSARIES
| NAME | YEAR | NAME | YEAR |
|------|------|------|------|
|      |      |      |      |
|      |      |      |      |

### SPECIAL EVENTS & MEMORIES
| EVENT | YEAR | EVENT | YEAR |
|-------|------|-------|------|
|       |      |       |      |
|       |      |       |      |
|       |      |       |      |

## JUNE 30

### BIRTHDAYS
| NAME | YEAR | NAME | YEAR |
|------|------|------|------|
|      |      |      |      |
|      |      |      |      |
|      |      |      |      |

### ANNIVERSARIES
| NAME | YEAR | NAME | YEAR |
|------|------|------|------|
|      |      |      |      |
|      |      |      |      |

### SPECIAL EVENTS & MEMORIES
| EVENT | YEAR | EVENT | YEAR |
|-------|------|-------|------|
|       |      |       |      |
|       |      |       |      |
|       |      |       |      |

## NOTES:

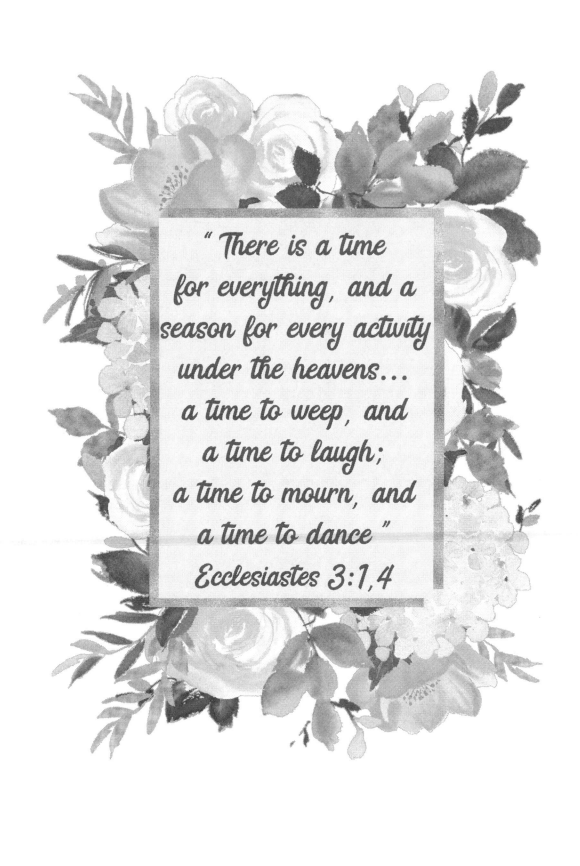

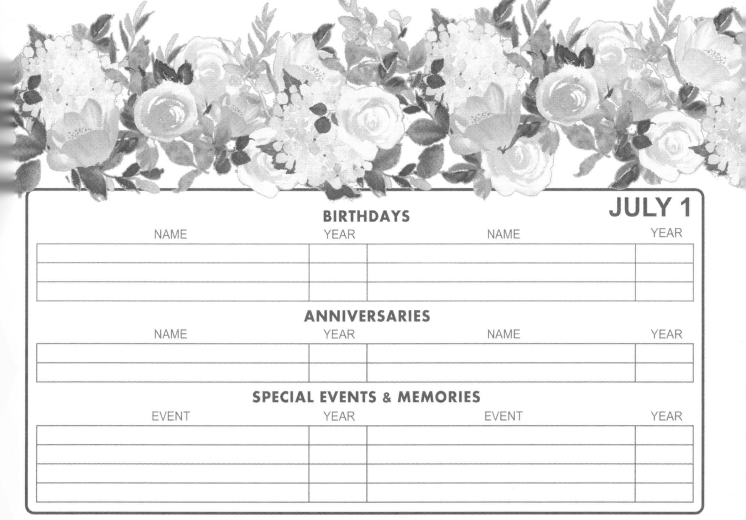

## JULY 1

### BIRTHDAYS
| NAME | YEAR | NAME | YEAR |
|---|---|---|---|
| | | | |
| | | | |
| | | | |

### ANNIVERSARIES
| NAME | YEAR | NAME | YEAR |
|---|---|---|---|
| | | | |
| | | | |

### SPECIAL EVENTS & MEMORIES
| EVENT | YEAR | EVENT | YEAR |
|---|---|---|---|
| | | | |
| | | | |
| | | | |
| | | | |

## JULY 2

### BIDAYS
| NAME | YEAR | NAME | YEAR |
|------|------|------|------|
|      |      |      |      |
|      |      |      |      |
|      |      |      |      |

### ANNIVERSARIES
| NAME | YEAR | NAME | YEAR |
|------|------|------|------|
|      |      |      |      |
|      |      |      |      |

### SPECIAL EVENTS & MEMORIES
| EVENT | YEAR | EVENT | YEAR |
|-------|------|-------|------|
|       |      |       |      |
|       |      |       |      |
|       |      |       |      |
|       |      |       |      |

## JULY 3

### BIRTHDAYS
| NAME | YEAR | NAME | YEAR |
|------|------|------|------|
|      |      |      |      |
|      |      |      |      |
|      |      |      |      |

### ANNIVERSARIES
| NAME | YEAR | NAME | YEAR |
|------|------|------|------|
|      |      |      |      |
|      |      |      |      |

### SPECIAL EVENTS & MEMORIES
| EVENT | YEAR | EVENT | YEAR |
|-------|------|-------|------|
|       |      |       |      |
|       |      |       |      |
|       |      |       |      |
|       |      |       |      |

## JULY 4

### BIRTHDAYS
| NAME | YEAR | NAME | YEAR |
|------|------|------|------|
| Brittany Elias | 1992 |  |  |
|      |      |      |      |
|      |      |      |      |

### ANNIVERSARIES
| NAME | YEAR | NAME | YEAR |
|------|------|------|------|
|      |      |      |      |
|      |      |      |      |

### SPECIAL EVENTS & MEMORIES
| EVENT | YEAR | EVENT | YEAR |
|-------|------|-------|------|
|       |      |       |      |
|       |      |       |      |
|       |      |       |      |
|       |      |       |      |

## JULY 5

### BIRTHDAYS
| NAME | YEAR | NAME | YEAR |
|---|---|---|---|
|  |  |  |  |
|  |  |  |  |
|  |  |  |  |

### ANNIVERSARIES
| NAME | YEAR | NAME | YEAR |
|---|---|---|---|
|  |  |  |  |
|  |  |  |  |

### SPECIAL EVENTS & MEMORIES
| EVENT | YEAR | EVENT | YEAR |
|---|---|---|---|
|  |  |  |  |
|  |  |  |  |
|  |  |  |  |
|  |  |  |  |

## JULY 6

### BIRTHDAYS
| NAME | YEAR | NAME | YEAR |
|---|---|---|---|
|  |  |  |  |
|  |  |  |  |
|  |  |  |  |

### ANNIVERSARIES
| NAME | YEAR | NAME | YEAR |
|---|---|---|---|
|  |  |  |  |
|  |  |  |  |

### SPECIAL EVENTS & MEMORIES
| EVENT | YEAR | EVENT | YEAR |
|---|---|---|---|
|  |  |  |  |
|  |  |  |  |
|  |  |  |  |
|  |  |  |  |

## JULY 7

### BIRTHDAYS
| NAME | YEAR | NAME | YEAR |
|---|---|---|---|
|  |  |  |  |
|  |  |  |  |
|  |  |  |  |

### ANNIVERSARIES
| NAME | YEAR | NAME | YEAR |
|---|---|---|---|
|  |  |  |  |
|  |  |  |  |

### SPECIAL EVENTS & MEMORIES
| EVENT | YEAR | EVENT | YEAR |
|---|---|---|---|
|  |  |  |  |
|  |  |  |  |
|  |  |  |  |
|  |  |  |  |

## JULY 8

### BIRTHDAYS
| NAME | YEAR | NAME | YEAR |
|------|------|------|------|
|      |      |      |      |
|      |      |      |      |

### ANNIVERSARIES
| NAME | YEAR | NAME | YEAR |
|------|------|------|------|
|      |      |      |      |
|      |      |      |      |

### SPECIAL EVENTS & MEMORIES
| EVENT | YEAR | EVENT | YEAR |
|-------|------|-------|------|
|       |      |       |      |
|       |      |       |      |
|       |      |       |      |

## JULY 9

### BIRTHDAYS
| NAME | YEAR | NAME | YEAR |
|------|------|------|------|
|      |      |      |      |
|      |      |      |      |
|      |      |      |      |

### ANNIVERSARIES
| NAME | YEAR | NAME | YEAR |
|------|------|------|------|
|      |      |      |      |
|      |      |      |      |

### SPECIAL EVENTS & MEMORIES
| EVENT | YEAR | EVENT | YEAR |
|-------|------|-------|------|
|       |      |       |      |
|       |      |       |      |
|       |      |       |      |

## JULY 10

### BIRTHDAYS
| NAME | YEAR | NAME | YEAR |
|------|------|------|------|
|      |      |      |      |
|      |      |      |      |
|      |      |      |      |

### ANNIVERSARIES
| NAME | YEAR | NAME | YEAR |
|------|------|------|------|
|      |      |      |      |
|      |      |      |      |

### SPECIAL EVENTS & MEMORIES
| EVENT | YEAR | EVENT | YEAR |
|-------|------|-------|------|
|       |      |       |      |
|       |      |       |      |
|       |      |       |      |

## JULY 11

### BIRTHDAYS
| NAME | YEAR | NAME | YEAR |
|---|---|---|---|
| | | | |
| | | | |

### ANNIVERSARIES
| NAME | YEAR | NAME | YEAR |
|---|---|---|---|
| | | | |
| | | | |

### SPECIAL EVENTS & MEMORIES
| EVENT | YEAR | EVENT | YEAR |
|---|---|---|---|
| | | | |
| | | | |
| | | | |

## JULY 12

### BIRTHDAYS
| NAME | YEAR | NAME | YEAR |
|---|---|---|---|
| | | | |
| | | | |

### ANNIVERSARIES
| NAME | YEAR | NAME | YEAR |
|---|---|---|---|
| | | | |
| | | | |

### SPECIAL EVENTS & MEMORIES
| EVENT | YEAR | EVENT | YEAR |
|---|---|---|---|
| | | | |
| | | | |
| | | | |

## JULY 13

### BIRTHDAYS
| NAME | YEAR | NAME | YEAR |
|---|---|---|---|
| | | | |
| | | | |

### ANNIVERSARIES
| NAME | YEAR | NAME | YEAR |
|---|---|---|---|
| | | | |
| | | | |

### SPECIAL EVENTS & MEMORIES
| EVENT | YEAR | EVENT | YEAR |
|---|---|---|---|
| | | | |
| | | | |
| | | | |

## JULY 14

### BIRTHDAYS
| NAME | YEAR | NAME | YEAR |
|---|---|---|---|
|  |  |  |  |
|  |  |  |  |

### ANNIVERSARIES
| NAME | YEAR | NAME | YEAR |
|---|---|---|---|
|  |  |  |  |

### SPECIAL EVENTS & MEMORIES
| EVENT | YEAR | EVENT | YEAR |
|---|---|---|---|
|  |  |  |  |
|  |  |  |  |
|  |  |  |  |

## JULY 15

### BIRTHDAYS
| NAME | YEAR | NAME | YEAR |
|---|---|---|---|
|  |  |  |  |
|  |  |  |  |

### ANNIVERSARIES
| NAME | YEAR | NAME | YEAR |
|---|---|---|---|
| Rick + Stacey Harris | 2016 |  |  |

### SPECIAL EVENTS & MEMORIES
| EVENT | YEAR | EVENT | YEAR |
|---|---|---|---|
|  |  |  |  |
|  |  |  |  |
|  |  |  |  |

## JULY 16

### BIRTHDAYS
| NAME | YEAR | NAME | YEAR |
|---|---|---|---|
|  |  |  |  |
|  |  |  |  |

### ANNIVERSARIES
| NAME | YEAR | NAME | YEAR |
|---|---|---|---|
|  |  |  |  |

### SPECIAL EVENTS & MEMORIES
| EVENT | YEAR | EVENT | YEAR |
|---|---|---|---|
|  |  |  |  |
|  |  |  |  |
|  |  |  |  |

## JULY 17

### BIRTHDAYS
| NAME | YEAR | NAME | YEAR |
|---|---|---|---|
|  |  |  |  |
|  |  |  |  |
|  |  |  |  |

### ANNIVERSARIES
| NAME | YEAR | NAME | YEAR |
|---|---|---|---|
|  |  |  |  |
|  |  |  |  |

### SPECIAL EVENTS & MEMORIES
| EVENT | YEAR | EVENT | YEAR |
|---|---|---|---|
|  |  |  |  |
|  |  |  |  |
|  |  |  |  |
|  |  |  |  |

## JULY 18

### BIRTHDAYS
| NAME | YEAR | NAME | YEAR |
|---|---|---|---|
|  |  |  |  |
|  |  |  |  |
|  |  |  |  |

### ANNIVERSARIES
| NAME | YEAR | NAME | YEAR |
|---|---|---|---|
|  |  |  |  |
|  |  |  |  |

### SPECIAL EVENTS & MEMORIES
| EVENT | YEAR | EVENT | YEAR |
|---|---|---|---|
|  |  |  |  |
|  |  |  |  |
|  |  |  |  |
|  |  |  |  |

## JULY 19

### BIRTHDAYS
| NAME | YEAR | NAME | YEAR |
|---|---|---|---|
| Mallory Staples |  |  |  |
|  |  |  |  |
|  |  |  |  |

### ANNIVERSARIES
| NAME | YEAR | NAME | YEAR |
|---|---|---|---|
|  |  |  |  |
|  |  |  |  |

### SPECIAL EVENTS & MEMORIES
| EVENT | YEAR | EVENT | YEAR |
|---|---|---|---|
|  |  |  |  |
|  |  |  |  |
|  |  |  |  |
|  |  |  |  |

## JULY 20

### BIRTHDAYS
| NAME | YEAR | NAME | YEAR |
|------|------|------|------|
|      |      |      |      |
|      |      |      |      |
|      |      |      |      |

### ANNIVERSARIES
| NAME | YEAR | NAME | YEAR |
|------|------|------|------|
|      |      |      |      |
|      |      |      |      |

### SPECIAL EVENTS & MEMORIES
| EVENT | YEAR | EVENT | YEAR |
|-------|------|-------|------|
|       |      |       |      |
|       |      |       |      |
|       |      |       |      |
|       |      |       |      |

## JULY 21

### BIRTHDAYS
| NAME | YEAR | NAME | YEAR |
|------|------|------|------|
|      |      |      |      |
|      |      |      |      |
|      |      |      |      |

### ANNIVERSARIES
| NAME | YEAR | NAME | YEAR |
|------|------|------|------|
|      |      |      |      |
|      |      |      |      |

### SPECIAL EVENTS & MEMORIES
| EVENT | YEAR | EVENT | YEAR |
|-------|------|-------|------|
|       |      |       |      |
|       |      |       |      |
|       |      |       |      |
|       |      |       |      |

## JULY 22

### BIRTHDAYS
| NAME | YEAR | NAME | YEAR |
|------|------|------|------|
|      |      |      |      |
|      |      |      |      |
|      |      |      |      |

### ANNIVERSARIES
| NAME | YEAR | NAME | YEAR |
|------|------|------|------|
|      |      |      |      |
|      |      |      |      |

### SPECIAL EVENTS & MEMORIES
| EVENT | YEAR | EVENT | YEAR |
|-------|------|-------|------|
|       |      |       |      |
|       |      |       |      |
|       |      |       |      |
|       |      |       |      |

## JULY 23

### BIRTHDAYS

| NAME | YEAR | NAME | YEAR |
|---|---|---|---|
| Raleigh George | 2002 | | |
| | | | |

### ANNIVERSARIES

| NAME | YEAR | NAME | YEAR |
|---|---|---|---|
| | | | |
| | | | |

### SPECIAL EVENTS & MEMORIES

| EVENT | YEAR | EVENT | YEAR |
|---|---|---|---|
| | | | |
| | | | |
| | | | |
| | | | |

## JULY 24

### BIRTHDAYS

| NAME | YEAR | NAME | YEAR |
|---|---|---|---|
| | | | |
| | | | |

### ANNIVERSARIES

| NAME | YEAR | NAME | YEAR |
|---|---|---|---|
| | | | |
| | | | |

### SPECIAL EVENTS & MEMORIES

| EVENT | YEAR | EVENT | YEAR |
|---|---|---|---|
| | | | |
| | | | |
| | | | |
| | | | |

## JULY 25

### BIRTHDAYS

| NAME | YEAR | NAME | YEAR |
|---|---|---|---|
| | | | |
| | | | |

### ANNIVERSARIES

| NAME | YEAR | NAME | YEAR |
|---|---|---|---|
| | | | |
| | | | |

### SPECIAL EVENTS & MEMORIES

| EVENT | YEAR | EVENT | YEAR |
|---|---|---|---|
| | | | |
| | | | |
| | | | |
| | | | |

## JULY 26

### BIRTHDAYS
| NAME | YEAR | NAME | YEAR |
|---|---|---|---|
| | | | |
| | | | |
| | | | |

### ANNIVERSARIES
| NAME | YEAR | NAME | YEAR |
|---|---|---|---|
| | | | |
| | | | |

### SPECIAL EVENTS & MEMORIES
| EVENT | YEAR | EVENT | YEAR |
|---|---|---|---|
| | | | |
| | | | |
| | | | |
| | | | |

## JULY 27

### BIRTHDAYS
| NAME | YEAR | NAME | YEAR |
|---|---|---|---|
| | | | |
| | | | |
| | | | |

### ANNIVERSARIES
| NAME | YEAR | NAME | YEAR |
|---|---|---|---|
| | | | |
| | | | |

### SPECIAL EVENTS & MEMORIES
| EVENT | YEAR | EVENT | YEAR |
|---|---|---|---|
| | | | |
| | | | |
| | | | |
| | | | |

## JULY 28

### BIRTHDAYS
| NAME | YEAR | NAME | YEAR |
|---|---|---|---|
| Joseph Nolan Elias | 2020 | | |
| Taylor Elias | | | |
| | | | |

### ANNIVERSARIES
| NAME | YEAR | NAME | YEAR |
|---|---|---|---|
| | | | |
| | | | |

### SPECIAL EVENTS & MEMORIES
| EVENT | YEAR | EVENT | YEAR |
|---|---|---|---|
| | | | |
| | | | |
| | | | |
| | | | |

## JULY 29

### BIRTHDAYS
| NAME | YEAR | NAME | YEAR |
|---|---|---|---|
|  |  |  |  |
|  |  |  |  |

### ANNIVERSARIES
| NAME | YEAR | NAME | YEAR |
|---|---|---|---|
|  |  |  |  |

### SPECIAL EVENTS & MEMORIES
| EVENT | YEAR | EVENT | YEAR |
|---|---|---|---|
|  |  |  |  |
|  |  |  |  |
|  |  |  |  |

## JULY 30

### BIRTHDAYS
| NAME | YEAR | NAME | YEAR |
|---|---|---|---|
|  |  |  |  |
|  |  |  |  |

### ANNIVERSARIES
| NAME | YEAR | NAME | YEAR |
|---|---|---|---|
|  |  |  |  |

### SPECIAL EVENTS & MEMORIES
| EVENT | YEAR | EVENT | YEAR |
|---|---|---|---|
|  |  |  |  |
|  |  |  |  |
|  |  |  |  |

## JULY 31

### BIRTHDAYS
| NAME | YEAR | NAME | YEAR |
|---|---|---|---|
|  |  |  |  |
|  |  |  |  |

### ANNIVERSARIES
| NAME | YEAR | NAME | YEAR |
|---|---|---|---|
|  |  |  |  |

### SPECIAL EVENTS & MEMORIES
| EVENT | YEAR | EVENT | YEAR |
|---|---|---|---|
|  |  |  |  |
|  |  |  |  |
|  |  |  |  |

## AUGUST 1

### BIRTHDAYS
| NAME | YEAR | NAME | YEAR |
|---|---|---|---|
|  |  |  |  |
|  |  |  |  |
|  |  |  |  |

### ANNIVERSARIES
| NAME | YEAR | NAME | YEAR |
|---|---|---|---|
|  |  |  |  |
|  |  |  |  |

### SPECIAL EVENTS & MEMORIES
| EVENT | YEAR | EVENT | YEAR |
|---|---|---|---|
|  |  |  |  |
|  |  |  |  |
|  |  |  |  |
|  |  |  |  |

# AUGUST 2

### BIRTHDAYS

| NAME | YEAR | NAME | YEAR |
|---|---|---|---|
|  |  |  |  |
|  |  |  |  |

### ANNIVERSARIES

| NAME | YEAR | NAME | YEAR |
|---|---|---|---|
|  |  |  |  |
|  |  |  |  |

### SPECIAL EVENTS & MEMORIES

| EVENT | YEAR | EVENT | YEAR |
|---|---|---|---|
|  |  |  |  |
|  |  |  |  |
|  |  |  |  |

# AUGUST 3

### BIRTHDAYS

| NAME | YEAR | NAME | YEAR |
|---|---|---|---|
| Parker Campigalia | 1998 |  |  |
|  |  |  |  |

### ANNIVERSARIES

| NAME | YEAR | NAME | YEAR |
|---|---|---|---|
|  |  |  |  |
|  |  |  |  |

### SPECIAL EVENTS & MEMORIES

| EVENT | YEAR | EVENT | YEAR |
|---|---|---|---|
|  |  |  |  |
|  |  |  |  |
|  |  |  |  |

# AUGUST 4

### BIRTHDAYS

| NAME | YEAR | NAME | YEAR |
|---|---|---|---|
|  |  |  |  |
|  |  |  |  |

### ANNIVERSARIES

| NAME | YEAR | NAME | YEAR |
|---|---|---|---|
|  |  |  |  |
|  |  |  |  |

### SPECIAL EVENTS & MEMORIES

| EVENT | YEAR | EVENT | YEAR |
|---|---|---|---|
|  |  |  |  |
|  |  |  |  |
|  |  |  |  |

# AUGUST 5

## BIRTHDAYS

| NAME | YEAR | NAME | YEAR |
|---|---|---|---|
| | | | |
| | | | |
| | | | |

## ANNIVERSARIES

| NAME | YEAR | NAME | YEAR |
|---|---|---|---|
| | | | |
| | | | |

## SPECIAL EVENTS & MEMORIES

| EVENT | YEAR | EVENT | YEAR |
|---|---|---|---|
| | | | |
| | | | |
| | | | |
| | | | |

# AUGUST 6

## BIRTHDAYS

| NAME | YEAR | NAME | YEAR |
|---|---|---|---|
| | | | |
| | | | |
| | | | |

## ANNIVERSARIES

| NAME | YEAR | NAME | YEAR |
|---|---|---|---|
| | | | |
| | | | |

## SPECIAL EVENTS & MEMORIES

| EVENT | YEAR | EVENT | YEAR |
|---|---|---|---|
| | | | |
| | | | |
| | | | |
| | | | |

# AUGUST 7

## BIRTHDAYS

| NAME | YEAR | NAME | YEAR |
|---|---|---|---|
| | | | |
| | | | |
| | | | |

## ANNIVERSARIES

| NAME | YEAR | NAME | YEAR |
|---|---|---|---|
| | | | |
| | | | |

## SPECIAL EVENTS & MEMORIES

| EVENT | YEAR | EVENT | YEAR |
|---|---|---|---|
| | | | |
| | | | |
| | | | |
| | | | |

# AUGUST 8

## BIRTHDAYS
| NAME | YEAR | NAME | YEAR |
|------|------|------|------|
|      |      |      |      |
|      |      |      |      |
|      |      |      |      |

## ANNIVERSARIES
| NAME | YEAR | NAME | YEAR |
|------|------|------|------|
|      |      |      |      |
|      |      |      |      |

## SPECIAL EVENTS & MEMORIES
| EVENT | YEAR | EVENT | YEAR |
|-------|------|-------|------|
|       |      |       |      |
|       |      |       |      |
|       |      |       |      |

# AUGUST 9

## BIRTHDAYS
| NAME | YEAR | NAME | YEAR |
|------|------|------|------|
|      |      |      |      |
|      |      |      |      |
|      |      |      |      |

## ANNIVERSARIES
| NAME | YEAR | NAME | YEAR |
|------|------|------|------|
|      |      |      |      |
|      |      |      |      |

## SPECIAL EVENTS & MEMORIES
| EVENT | YEAR | EVENT | YEAR |
|-------|------|-------|------|
|       |      |       |      |
|       |      |       |      |
|       |      |       |      |

# AUGUST 10

## BIRTHDAYS
| NAME | YEAR | NAME | YEAR |
|------|------|------|------|
|      |      |      |      |
|      |      |      |      |
|      |      |      |      |

## ANNIVERSARIES
| NAME | YEAR | NAME | YEAR |
|------|------|------|------|
|      |      |      |      |
|      |      |      |      |

## SPECIAL EVENTS & MEMORIES
| EVENT | YEAR | EVENT | YEAR |
|-------|------|-------|------|
|       |      |       |      |
|       |      |       |      |
|       |      |       |      |

# AUGUST 11

## BIRTHDAYS

| NAME | YEAR | NAME | YEAR |
|---|---|---|---|
| | | | |
| | | | |
| | | | |

## ANNIVERSARIES

| NAME | YEAR | NAME | YEAR |
|---|---|---|---|
| | | | |
| | | | |

## SPECIAL EVENTS & MEMORIES

| EVENT | YEAR | EVENT | YEAR |
|---|---|---|---|
| | | | |
| | | | |
| | | | |
| | | | |

# AUGUST 12

## BIRTHDAYS

| NAME | YEAR | NAME | YEAR |
|---|---|---|---|
| | | | |
| | | | |
| | | | |

## ANNIVERSARIES

| NAME | YEAR | NAME | YEAR |
|---|---|---|---|
| | | | |
| | | | |

## SPECIAL EVENTS & MEMORIES

| EVENT | YEAR | EVENT | YEAR |
|---|---|---|---|
| | | | |
| | | | |
| | | | |
| | | | |

# AUGUST 13

## BIRTHDAYS

| NAME | YEAR | NAME | YEAR |
|---|---|---|---|
| | | | |
| | | | |
| | | | |

## ANNIVERSARIES

| NAME | YEAR | NAME | YEAR |
|---|---|---|---|
| | | | |
| | | | |

## SPECIAL EVENTS & MEMORIES

| EVENT | YEAR | EVENT | YEAR |
|---|---|---|---|
| | | | |
| | | | |
| | | | |
| | | | |

## AUGUST 14

**BIRTHDAYS**

| NAME | YEAR | NAME | YEAR |
|------|------|------|------|
|  |  |  |  |
|  |  |  |  |
|  |  |  |  |

**ANNIVERSARIES**

| NAME | YEAR | NAME | YEAR |
|------|------|------|------|
|  |  |  |  |
|  |  |  |  |

**SPECIAL EVENTS & MEMORIES**

| EVENT | YEAR | EVENT | YEAR |
|-------|------|-------|------|
|  |  |  |  |
|  |  |  |  |
|  |  |  |  |
|  |  |  |  |

## AUGUST 15

**BIRTHDAYS**

| NAME | YEAR | NAME | YEAR |
|------|------|------|------|
|  |  |  |  |
|  |  |  |  |
|  |  |  |  |

**ANNIVERSARIES**

| NAME | YEAR | NAME | YEAR |
|------|------|------|------|
|  |  |  |  |
|  |  |  |  |

**SPECIAL EVENTS & MEMORIES**

| EVENT | YEAR | EVENT | YEAR |
|-------|------|-------|------|
|  |  |  |  |
|  |  |  |  |
|  |  |  |  |
|  |  |  |  |

## AUGUST 16

**BIRTHDAYS**

| NAME | YEAR | NAME | YEAR |
|------|------|------|------|
|  |  |  |  |
|  |  |  |  |
|  |  |  |  |

**ANNIVERSARIES**

| NAME | YEAR | NAME | YEAR |
|------|------|------|------|
|  |  |  |  |
|  |  |  |  |

**SPECIAL EVENTS & MEMORIES**

| EVENT | YEAR | EVENT | YEAR |
|-------|------|-------|------|
|  |  |  |  |
|  |  |  |  |
|  |  |  |  |
|  |  |  |  |

## AUGUST 17

### BIRTHDAYS
| NAME | YEAR | NAME | YEAR |
|------|------|------|------|
|      |      |      |      |
|      |      |      |      |
|      |      |      |      |

### ANNIVERSARIES
| NAME | YEAR | NAME | YEAR |
|------|------|------|------|
|      |      |      |      |
|      |      |      |      |

### SPECIAL EVENTS & MEMORIES
| EVENT | YEAR | EVENT | YEAR |
|-------|------|-------|------|
|       |      |       |      |
|       |      |       |      |
|       |      |       |      |
|       |      |       |      |

## AUGUST 18

### BIRTHDAYS
| NAME | YEAR | NAME | YEAR |
|------|------|------|------|
|      |      |      |      |
|      |      |      |      |
|      |      |      |      |

### ANNIVERSARIES
| NAME | YEAR | NAME | YEAR |
|------|------|------|------|
|      |      |      |      |
|      |      |      |      |

### SPECIAL EVENTS & MEMORIES
| EVENT | YEAR | EVENT | YEAR |
|-------|------|-------|------|
|       |      |       |      |
|       |      |       |      |
|       |      |       |      |
|       |      |       |      |

## AUGUST 19

### BIRTHDAYS
| NAME | YEAR | NAME | YEAR |
|------|------|------|------|
| Malinda Jernigan |      |      |      |
|      |      |      |      |
|      |      |      |      |

### ANNIVERSARIES
| NAME | YEAR | NAME | YEAR |
|------|------|------|------|
|      |      |      |      |
|      |      |      |      |

### SPECIAL EVENTS & MEMORIES
| EVENT | YEAR | EVENT | YEAR |
|-------|------|-------|------|
|       |      |       |      |
|       |      |       |      |
|       |      |       |      |
|       |      |       |      |

# AUGUST 20

## BIRTHDAYS
| NAME | YEAR | NAME | YEAR |
|---|---|---|---|
| | | | |
| | | | |

## ANNIVERSARIES
| NAME | YEAR | NAME | YEAR |
|---|---|---|---|
| | | | |
| | | | |

## SPECIAL EVENTS & MEMORIES
| EVENT | YEAR | EVENT | YEAR |
|---|---|---|---|
| | | | |
| | | | |
| | | | |
| | | | |

# AUGUST 21

## BIRTHDAYS
| NAME | YEAR | NAME | YEAR |
|---|---|---|---|
| | | | |
| | | | |

## ANNIVERSARIES
| NAME | YEAR | NAME | YEAR |
|---|---|---|---|
| | | | |
| | | | |

## SPECIAL EVENTS & MEMORIES
| EVENT | YEAR | EVENT | YEAR |
|---|---|---|---|
| | | | |
| | | | |
| | | | |
| | | | |

# AUGUST 22

## BIRTHDAYS
| NAME | YEAR | NAME | YEAR |
|---|---|---|---|
| | | | |
| | | | |

## ANNIVERSARIES
| NAME | YEAR | NAME | YEAR |
|---|---|---|---|
| | | | |
| | | | |

## SPECIAL EVENTS & MEMORIES
| EVENT | YEAR | EVENT | YEAR |
|---|---|---|---|
| | | | |
| | | | |
| | | | |
| | | | |

# AUGUST 23

## BIRTHDAYS
| NAME | YEAR | NAME | YEAR |
|---|---|---|---|
| | | | |
| | | | |
| | | | |

## ANNIVERSARIES
| NAME | YEAR | NAME | YEAR |
|---|---|---|---|
| | | | |
| | | | |

## SPECIAL EVENTS & MEMORIES
| EVENT | YEAR | EVENT | YEAR |
|---|---|---|---|
| | | | |
| | | | |
| | | | |
| | | | |

# AUGUST 24

## BIRTHDAYS
| NAME | YEAR | NAME | YEAR |
|---|---|---|---|
| | | | |
| | | | |
| | | | |

## ANNIVERSARIES
| NAME | YEAR | NAME | YEAR |
|---|---|---|---|
| | | | |
| | | | |

## SPECIAL EVENTS & MEMORIES
| EVENT | YEAR | EVENT | YEAR |
|---|---|---|---|
| | | | |
| | | | |
| | | | |
| | | | |

# AUGUST 25

## BIRTHDAYS
| NAME | YEAR | NAME | YEAR |
|---|---|---|---|
| | | | |
| | | | |
| | | | |

## ANNIVERSARIES
| NAME | YEAR | NAME | YEAR |
|---|---|---|---|
| | | | |
| | | | |

## SPECIAL EVENTS & MEMORIES
| EVENT | YEAR | EVENT | YEAR |
|---|---|---|---|
| | | | |
| | | | |
| | | | |
| | | | |

# AUGUST 26

### BIRTHDAYS
| NAME | YEAR | NAME | YEAR |
|---|---|---|---|
|  |  |  |  |
|  |  |  |  |

### ANNIVERSARIES
| NAME | YEAR | NAME | YEAR |
|---|---|---|---|
|  |  |  |  |
|  |  |  |  |

### SPECIAL EVENTS & MEMORIES
| EVENT | YEAR | EVENT | YEAR |
|---|---|---|---|
|  |  |  |  |
|  |  |  |  |
|  |  |  |  |

# AUGUST 27

### BIRTHDAYS
| NAME | YEAR | NAME | YEAR |
|---|---|---|---|
|  |  |  |  |
|  |  |  |  |

### ANNIVERSARIES
| NAME | YEAR | NAME | YEAR |
|---|---|---|---|
|  |  |  |  |
|  |  |  |  |

### SPECIAL EVENTS & MEMORIES
| EVENT | YEAR | EVENT | YEAR |
|---|---|---|---|
|  |  |  |  |
|  |  |  |  |
|  |  |  |  |

# AUGUST 28

### BIRTHDAYS
| NAME | YEAR | NAME | YEAR |
|---|---|---|---|
|  |  |  |  |
|  |  |  |  |

### ANNIVERSARIES
| NAME | YEAR | NAME | YEAR |
|---|---|---|---|
|  |  |  |  |
|  |  |  |  |

### SPECIAL EVENTS & MEMORIES
| EVENT | YEAR | EVENT | YEAR |
|---|---|---|---|
|  |  |  |  |
|  |  |  |  |
|  |  |  |  |

# AUGUST 29

## BIRTHDAYS

| NAME | YEAR | NAME | YEAR |
|---|---|---|---|
|  |  |  |  |
|  |  |  |  |
|  |  |  |  |

## ANNIVERSARIES

| NAME | YEAR | NAME | YEAR |
|---|---|---|---|
|  |  |  |  |
|  |  |  |  |

## SPECIAL EVENTS & MEMORIES

| EVENT | YEAR | EVENT | YEAR |
|---|---|---|---|
|  |  |  |  |
|  |  |  |  |
|  |  |  |  |
|  |  |  |  |

# AUGUST 30

## BIRTHDAYS

| NAME | YEAR | NAME | YEAR |
|---|---|---|---|
| Luke Thoup |  |  |  |
|  |  |  |  |
|  |  |  |  |

## ANNIVERSARIES

| NAME | YEAR | NAME | YEAR |
|---|---|---|---|
|  |  |  |  |
|  |  |  |  |

## SPECIAL EVENTS & MEMORIES

| EVENT | YEAR | EVENT | YEAR |
|---|---|---|---|
|  |  |  |  |
|  |  |  |  |
|  |  |  |  |
|  |  |  |  |

# AUGUST 31

## BIRTHDAYS

| NAME | YEAR | NAME | YEAR |
|---|---|---|---|
|  |  |  |  |
|  |  |  |  |
|  |  |  |  |

## ANNIVERSARIES

| NAME | YEAR | NAME | YEAR |
|---|---|---|---|
|  |  |  |  |
|  |  |  |  |

## SPECIAL EVENTS & MEMORIES

| EVENT | YEAR | EVENT | YEAR |
|---|---|---|---|
|  |  |  |  |
|  |  |  |  |
|  |  |  |  |
|  |  |  |  |

## SEPTEMBER 1

### BIRTHDAYS

| NAME | YEAR | NAME | YEAR |
|------|------|------|------|
|      |      |      |      |
|      |      |      |      |
|      |      |      |      |

### ANNIVERSARIES

| NAME | YEAR | NAME | YEAR |
|------|------|------|------|
|      |      |      |      |
|      |      |      |      |

### SPECIAL EVENTS & MEMORIES

| EVENT | YEAR | EVENT | YEAR |
|-------|------|-------|------|
|       |      |       |      |
|       |      |       |      |
|       |      |       |      |
|       |      |       |      |

# SEPTEMBER 2

**BIRTHDAYS**

| NAME | YEAR | NAME | YEAR |
|------|------|------|------|
|      |      |      |      |
|      |      |      |      |

**ANNIVERSARIES**

| NAME | YEAR | NAME | YEAR |
|------|------|------|------|
|      |      |      |      |
|      |      |      |      |

**SPECIAL EVENTS & MEMORIES**

| EVENT | YEAR | EVENT | YEAR |
|-------|------|-------|------|
|       |      |       |      |
|       |      |       |      |
|       |      |       |      |

# SEPTEMBER 3

**BIRTHDAYS**

| NAME | YEAR | NAME | YEAR |
|------|------|------|------|
| Coachie | 1948 |   |   |
|      |      |      |      |

**ANNIVERSARIES**

| NAME | YEAR | NAME | YEAR |
|------|------|------|------|
|      |      |      |      |
|      |      |      |      |

**SPECIAL EVENTS & MEMORIES**

| EVENT | YEAR | EVENT | YEAR |
|-------|------|-------|------|
|       |      |       |      |
|       |      |       |      |
|       |      |       |      |

# SEPTEMBER 4

**BIRTHDAYS**

| NAME | YEAR | NAME | YEAR |
|------|------|------|------|
|      |      |      |      |
|      |      |      |      |

**ANNIVERSARIES**

| NAME | YEAR | NAME | YEAR |
|------|------|------|------|
|      |      |      |      |
|      |      |      |      |

**SPECIAL EVENTS & MEMORIES**

| EVENT | YEAR | EVENT | YEAR |
|-------|------|-------|------|
|       |      |       |      |
|       |      |       |      |
|       |      |       |      |

# SEPTEMBER 5

## BIRTHDAYS
| NAME | YEAR | NAME | YEAR |
|------|------|------|------|
|      |      |      |      |
|      |      |      |      |
|      |      |      |      |

## ANNIVERSARIES
| NAME | YEAR | NAME | YEAR |
|------|------|------|------|
|      |      |      |      |
|      |      |      |      |

## SPECIAL EVENTS & MEMORIES
| EVENT | YEAR | EVENT | YEAR |
|-------|------|-------|------|
|       |      |       |      |
|       |      |       |      |
|       |      |       |      |
|       |      |       |      |

# SEPTEMBER 6

## BIRTHDAYS
| NAME | YEAR | NAME | YEAR |
|------|------|------|------|
| Lea Olszeski | 2001 | | |
|      |      |      |      |
|      |      |      |      |

## ANNIVERSARIES
| NAME | YEAR | NAME | YEAR |
|------|------|------|------|
|      |      |      |      |
|      |      |      |      |

## SPECIAL EVENTS & MEMORIES
| EVENT | YEAR | EVENT | YEAR |
|-------|------|-------|------|
|       |      |       |      |
|       |      |       |      |
|       |      |       |      |
|       |      |       |      |

# SEPTEMBER 7

## BIRTHDAYS
| NAME | YEAR | NAME | YEAR |
|------|------|------|------|
|      |      |      |      |
|      |      |      |      |
|      |      |      |      |

## ANNIVERSARIES
| NAME | YEAR | NAME | YEAR |
|------|------|------|------|
|      |      |      |      |
|      |      |      |      |

## SPECIAL EVENTS & MEMORIES
| EVENT | YEAR | EVENT | YEAR |
|-------|------|-------|------|
|       |      |       |      |
|       |      |       |      |
|       |      |       |      |
|       |      |       |      |

# SEPTEMBER 8

## BIRTHDAYS

| NAME | YEAR | NAME | YEAR |
|------|------|------|------|
|      |      |      |      |
|      |      |      |      |
|      |      |      |      |

## ANNIVERSARIES

| NAME | YEAR | NAME | YEAR |
|------|------|------|------|
|      |      |      |      |
|      |      |      |      |

## SPECIAL EVENTS & MEMORIES

| EVENT | YEAR | EVENT | YEAR |
|-------|------|-------|------|
|       |      |       |      |
|       |      |       |      |
|       |      |       |      |
|       |      |       |      |

# SEPTEMBER 9

## BIRTHDAYS

| NAME | YEAR | NAME | YEAR |
|------|------|------|------|
|      |      |      |      |
|      |      |      |      |
|      |      |      |      |

## ANNIVERSARIES

| NAME | YEAR | NAME | YEAR |
|------|------|------|------|
|      |      |      |      |
|      |      |      |      |

## SPECIAL EVENTS & MEMORIES

| EVENT | YEAR | EVENT | YEAR |
|-------|------|-------|------|
|       |      |       |      |
|       |      |       |      |
|       |      |       |      |
|       |      |       |      |

# SEPTEMBER 10

## BIRTHDAYS

| NAME | YEAR | NAME | YEAR |
|------|------|------|------|
|      |      |      |      |
|      |      |      |      |
|      |      |      |      |

## ANNIVERSARIES

| NAME | YEAR | NAME | YEAR |
|------|------|------|------|
|      |      |      |      |
|      |      |      |      |

## SPECIAL EVENTS & MEMORIES

| EVENT | YEAR | EVENT | YEAR |
|-------|------|-------|------|
|       |      |       |      |
|       |      |       |      |
|       |      |       |      |
|       |      |       |      |

## SEPTEMBER 11

### BIRTHDAYS
| NAME | YEAR | NAME | YEAR |
|------|------|------|------|
|  |  |  |  |
|  |  |  |  |
|  |  |  |  |

### ANNIVERSARIES
| NAME | YEAR | NAME | YEAR |
|------|------|------|------|
|  |  |  |  |
|  |  |  |  |

### SPECIAL EVENTS & MEMORIES
| EVENT | YEAR | EVENT | YEAR |
|-------|------|-------|------|
|  |  |  |  |
|  |  |  |  |
|  |  |  |  |
|  |  |  |  |

## SEPTEMBER 12

### BIRTHDAYS
| NAME | YEAR | NAME | YEAR |
|------|------|------|------|
| Julie Poland |  |  |  |
|  |  |  |  |
|  |  |  |  |

### ANNIVERSARIES
| NAME | YEAR | NAME | YEAR |
|------|------|------|------|
|  |  |  |  |
|  |  |  |  |

### SPECIAL EVENTS & MEMORIES
| EVENT | YEAR | EVENT | YEAR |
|-------|------|-------|------|
|  |  |  |  |
|  |  |  |  |
|  |  |  |  |
|  |  |  |  |

## SEPTEMBER 13

### BIRTHDAYS
| NAME | YEAR | NAME | YEAR |
|------|------|------|------|
|  |  |  |  |
|  |  |  |  |
|  |  |  |  |

### ANNIVERSARIES
| NAME | YEAR | NAME | YEAR |
|------|------|------|------|
|  |  |  |  |
|  |  |  |  |

### SPECIAL EVENTS & MEMORIES
| EVENT | YEAR | EVENT | YEAR |
|-------|------|-------|------|
|  |  |  |  |
|  |  |  |  |
|  |  |  |  |
|  |  |  |  |

## SEPTEMBER 14

**BIRTHDAYS**

| NAME | YEAR | NAME | YEAR |
|---|---|---|---|
| Hope & Duncan | 1999 | | |
| | | | |

**ANNIVERSARIES**

| NAME | YEAR | NAME | YEAR |
|---|---|---|---|
| | | | |
| | | | |

**SPECIAL EVENTS & MEMORIES**

| EVENT | YEAR | EVENT | YEAR |
|---|---|---|---|
| | | | |
| | | | |
| | | | |

## SEPTEMBER 15

**BIRTHDAYS**

| NAME | YEAR | NAME | YEAR |
|---|---|---|---|
| | | | |
| | | | |

**ANNIVERSARIES**

| NAME | YEAR | NAME | YEAR |
|---|---|---|---|
| | | | |
| | | | |

**SPECIAL EVENTS & MEMORIES**

| EVENT | YEAR | EVENT | YEAR |
|---|---|---|---|
| | | | |
| | | | |
| | | | |

## SEPTEMBER 16

**BIRTHDAYS**

| NAME | YEAR | NAME | YEAR |
|---|---|---|---|
| Morgan Gittings | 2000 | | |
| | | | |

**ANNIVERSARIES**

| NAME | YEAR | NAME | YEAR |
|---|---|---|---|
| | | | |
| | | | |

**SPECIAL EVENTS & MEMORIES**

| EVENT | YEAR | EVENT | YEAR |
|---|---|---|---|
| | | | |
| | | | |
| | | | |

# SEPTEMBER 17

## BIRTHDAYS
| NAME | YEAR | NAME | YEAR |
|---|---|---|---|
|  |  |  |  |
|  |  |  |  |
|  |  |  |  |

## ANNIVERSARIES
| NAME | YEAR | NAME | YEAR |
|---|---|---|---|
|  |  |  |  |
|  |  |  |  |

## SPECIAL EVENTS & MEMORIES
| EVENT | YEAR | EVENT | YEAR |
|---|---|---|---|
|  |  |  |  |
|  |  |  |  |
|  |  |  |  |
|  |  |  |  |

# SEPTEMBER 18

## BIRTHDAYS
| NAME | YEAR | NAME | YEAR |
|---|---|---|---|
|  |  |  |  |
|  |  |  |  |
|  |  |  |  |

## ANNIVERSARIES
| NAME | YEAR | NAME | YEAR |
|---|---|---|---|
|  |  |  |  |
|  |  |  |  |

## SPECIAL EVENTS & MEMORIES
| EVENT | YEAR | EVENT | YEAR |
|---|---|---|---|
|  |  |  |  |
|  |  |  |  |
|  |  |  |  |
|  |  |  |  |

# SEPTEMBER 19

## BIRTHDAYS
| NAME | YEAR | NAME | YEAR |
|---|---|---|---|
|  |  |  |  |
|  |  |  |  |
|  |  |  |  |

## ANNIVERSARIES
| NAME | YEAR | NAME | YEAR |
|---|---|---|---|
|  |  |  |  |
|  |  |  |  |

## SPECIAL EVENTS & MEMORIES
| EVENT | YEAR | EVENT | YEAR |
|---|---|---|---|
|  |  |  |  |
|  |  |  |  |
|  |  |  |  |
|  |  |  |  |

# SEPTEMBER 20

## BIRTHDAYS
| NAME | YEAR | NAME | YEAR |
|---|---|---|---|
| | | | |
| | | | |
| | | | |

## ANNIVERSARIES
| NAME | YEAR | NAME | YEAR |
|---|---|---|---|
| | | | |
| | | | |

## SPECIAL EVENTS & MEMORIES
| EVENT | YEAR | EVENT | YEAR |
|---|---|---|---|
| | | | |
| | | | |
| | | | |
| | | | |

# SEPTEMBER 21

## BIRTHDAYS
| NAME | YEAR | NAME | YEAR |
|---|---|---|---|
| | | | |
| | | | |
| | | | |

## ANNIVERSARIES
| NAME | YEAR | NAME | YEAR |
|---|---|---|---|
| | | | |
| | | | |

## SPECIAL EVENTS & MEMORIES
| EVENT | YEAR | EVENT | YEAR |
|---|---|---|---|
| | | | |
| | | | |
| | | | |
| | | | |

# SEPTEMBER 22

## BIRTHDAYS
| NAME | YEAR | NAME | YEAR |
|---|---|---|---|
| | | | |
| | | | |
| | | | |

## ANNIVERSARIES
| NAME | YEAR | NAME | YEAR |
|---|---|---|---|
| | | | |
| | | | |

## SPECIAL EVENTS & MEMORIES
| EVENT | YEAR | EVENT | YEAR |
|---|---|---|---|
| | | | |
| | | | |
| | | | |
| | | | |

# SEPTEMBER 23

## BIRTHDAYS

| NAME | YEAR | NAME | YEAR |
|---|---|---|---|
|  |  |  |  |
|  |  |  |  |
|  |  |  |  |

## ANNIVERSARIES

| NAME | YEAR | NAME | YEAR |
|---|---|---|---|
|  |  |  |  |
|  |  |  |  |

## SPECIAL EVENTS & MEMORIES

| EVENT | YEAR | EVENT | YEAR |
|---|---|---|---|
|  |  |  |  |
|  |  |  |  |
|  |  |  |  |
|  |  |  |  |

# SEPTEMBER 24

## BIRTHDAYS

| NAME | YEAR | NAME | YEAR |
|---|---|---|---|
|  |  |  |  |
|  |  |  |  |
|  |  |  |  |

## ANNIVERSARIES

| NAME | YEAR | NAME | YEAR |
|---|---|---|---|
|  |  |  |  |
|  |  |  |  |

## SPECIAL EVENTS & MEMORIES

| EVENT | YEAR | EVENT | YEAR |
|---|---|---|---|
|  |  |  |  |
|  |  |  |  |
|  |  |  |  |
|  |  |  |  |

# SEPTEMBER 25

## BIRTHDAYS

| NAME | YEAR | NAME | YEAR |
|---|---|---|---|
|  |  |  |  |
|  |  |  |  |
|  |  |  |  |

## ANNIVERSARIES

| NAME | YEAR | NAME | YEAR |
|---|---|---|---|
|  |  |  |  |
|  |  |  |  |

## SPECIAL EVENTS & MEMORIES

| EVENT | YEAR | EVENT | YEAR |
|---|---|---|---|
|  |  |  |  |
|  |  |  |  |
|  |  |  |  |
|  |  |  |  |

## SEPTEMBER 26

### BIRTHDAYS

| NAME | YEAR | NAME | YEAR |
|------|------|------|------|
|      |      |      |      |
|      |      |      |      |

### ANNIVERSARIES

| NAME | YEAR | NAME | YEAR |
|------|------|------|------|
|      |      |      |      |
|      |      |      |      |

### SPECIAL EVENTS & MEMORIES

| EVENT | YEAR | EVENT | YEAR |
|-------|------|-------|------|
|       |      |       |      |
|       |      |       |      |
|       |      |       |      |

## SEPTEMBER 27

### BIRTHDAYS

| NAME | YEAR | NAME | YEAR |
|------|------|------|------|
|      |      |      |      |
|      |      |      |      |

### ANNIVERSARIES

| NAME | YEAR | NAME | YEAR |
|------|------|------|------|
|      |      |      |      |
|      |      |      |      |

### SPECIAL EVENTS & MEMORIES

| EVENT | YEAR | EVENT | YEAR |
|-------|------|-------|------|
|       |      |       |      |
|       |      |       |      |
|       |      |       |      |

## SEPTEMBER 28

### BIRTHDAYS

| NAME | YEAR | NAME | YEAR |
|------|------|------|------|
|      |      |      |      |
|      |      |      |      |

### ANNIVERSARIES

| NAME | YEAR | NAME | YEAR |
|------|------|------|------|
|      |      |      |      |
|      |      |      |      |

### SPECIAL EVENTS & MEMORIES

| EVENT | YEAR | EVENT | YEAR |
|-------|------|-------|------|
|       |      |       |      |
|       |      |       |      |
|       |      |       |      |

## SEPTEMBER 29

**BIRTHDAYS**

| NAME | YEAR | NAME | YEAR |
|------|------|------|------|
|      |      |      |      |
|      |      |      |      |
|      |      |      |      |

**ANNIVERSARIES**

| NAME | YEAR | NAME | YEAR |
|------|------|------|------|
|      |      |      |      |
|      |      |      |      |

**SPECIAL EVENTS & MEMORIES**

| EVENT | YEAR | EVENT | YEAR |
|-------|------|-------|------|
|       |      |       |      |
|       |      |       |      |
|       |      |       |      |
|       |      |       |      |

## SEPTEMBER 30

**BIRTHDAYS**

| NAME | YEAR | NAME | YEAR |
|------|------|------|------|
|      |      |      |      |
|      |      |      |      |
|      |      |      |      |

**ANNIVERSARIES**

| NAME | YEAR | NAME | YEAR |
|------|------|------|------|
|      |      |      |      |
|      |      |      |      |

**SPECIAL EVENTS & MEMORIES**

| EVENT | YEAR | EVENT | YEAR |
|-------|------|-------|------|
|       |      |       |      |
|       |      |       |      |
|       |      |       |      |
|       |      |       |      |

## NOTES:

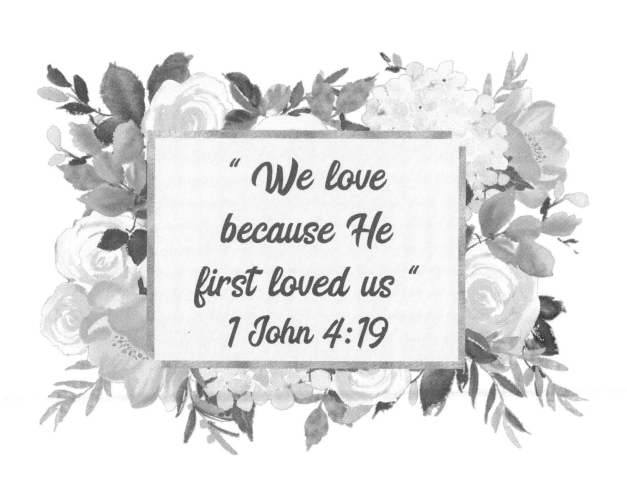

# OCTOBER 1

### BIRTHDAYS

| NAME | YEAR | NAME | YEAR |
|---|---|---|---|
|  |  |  |  |
|  |  |  |  |
|  |  |  |  |

### ANNIVERSARIES

| NAME | YEAR | NAME | YEAR |
|---|---|---|---|
|  |  |  |  |
|  |  |  |  |

### SPECIAL EVENTS & MEMORIES

| EVENT | YEAR | EVENT | YEAR |
|---|---|---|---|
|  |  |  |  |
|  |  |  |  |
|  |  |  |  |
|  |  |  |  |

# OCTOBER 2

**BIRTHDAYS**

| NAME | YEAR | NAME | YEAR |
|---|---|---|---|
| | | | |
| | | | |
| | | | |

**ANNIVERSARIES**

| NAME | YEAR | NAME | YEAR |
|---|---|---|---|
| | | | |
| | | | |

**SPECIAL EVENTS & MEMORIES**

| EVENT | YEAR | EVENT | YEAR |
|---|---|---|---|
| | | | |
| | | | |
| | | | |

# OCTOBER 3

**BIRTHDAYS**

| NAME | YEAR | NAME | YEAR |
|---|---|---|---|
| | | | |
| | | | |
| | | | |

**ANNIVERSARIES**

| NAME | YEAR | NAME | YEAR |
|---|---|---|---|
| | | | |
| | | | |

**SPECIAL EVENTS & MEMORIES**

| EVENT | YEAR | EVENT | YEAR |
|---|---|---|---|
| | | | |
| | | | |
| | | | |

# OCTOBER 4

**BIRTHDAYS**

| NAME | YEAR | NAME | YEAR |
|---|---|---|---|
| | | | |
| | | | |
| | | | |

**ANNIVERSARIES**

| NAME | YEAR | NAME | YEAR |
|---|---|---|---|
| | | | |
| | | | |

**SPECIAL EVENTS & MEMORIES**

| EVENT | YEAR | EVENT | YEAR |
|---|---|---|---|
| | | | |
| | | | |
| | | | |

# OCTOBER 5

## BIRTHDAYS

| NAME | YEAR | NAME | YEAR |
|---|---|---|---|
|  |  |  |  |
|  |  |  |  |

## ANNIVERSARIES

| NAME | YEAR | NAME | YEAR |
|---|---|---|---|
|  |  |  |  |
|  |  |  |  |

## SPECIAL EVENTS & MEMORIES

| EVENT | YEAR | EVENT | YEAR |
|---|---|---|---|
|  |  |  |  |
|  |  |  |  |
|  |  |  |  |
|  |  |  |  |

# OCTOBER 6

## BIRTHDAYS

| NAME | YEAR | NAME | YEAR |
|---|---|---|---|
|  |  |  |  |
|  |  |  |  |

## ANNIVERSARIES

| NAME | YEAR | NAME | YEAR |
|---|---|---|---|
|  |  |  |  |
|  |  |  |  |

## SPECIAL EVENTS & MEMORIES

| EVENT | YEAR | EVENT | YEAR |
|---|---|---|---|
|  |  |  |  |
|  |  |  |  |
|  |  |  |  |
|  |  |  |  |

# OCTOBER 7

## BIRTHDAYS

| NAME | YEAR | NAME | YEAR |
|---|---|---|---|
|  |  |  |  |
|  |  |  |  |

## ANNIVERSARIES

| NAME | YEAR | NAME | YEAR |
|---|---|---|---|
|  |  |  |  |
|  |  |  |  |

## SPECIAL EVENTS & MEMORIES

| EVENT | YEAR | EVENT | YEAR |
|---|---|---|---|
|  |  |  |  |
|  |  |  |  |
|  |  |  |  |
|  |  |  |  |

## OCTOBER 8

**BIRTHDAYS**

| NAME | YEAR | NAME | YEAR |
|---|---|---|---|
| | | | |
| | | | |
| | | | |

**ANNIVERSARIES**

| NAME | YEAR | NAME | YEAR |
|---|---|---|---|
| | | | |
| | | | |

**SPECIAL EVENTS & MEMORIES**

| EVENT | YEAR | EVENT | YEAR |
|---|---|---|---|
| | | | |
| | | | |
| | | | |

## OCTOBER 9

**BIRTHDAYS**

| NAME | YEAR | NAME | YEAR |
|---|---|---|---|
| | | | |
| | | | |
| | | | |

**ANNIVERSARIES**

| NAME | YEAR | NAME | YEAR |
|---|---|---|---|
| | | | |
| | | | |

**SPECIAL EVENTS & MEMORIES**

| EVENT | YEAR | EVENT | YEAR |
|---|---|---|---|
| | | | |
| | | | |
| | | | |

## OCTOBER 10

**BIRTHDAYS**

| NAME | YEAR | NAME | YEAR |
|---|---|---|---|
| Lee Lee Bryant | | | |
| | | | |
| | | | |

**ANNIVERSARIES**

| NAME | YEAR | NAME | YEAR |
|---|---|---|---|
| | | | |
| | | | |

**SPECIAL EVENTS & MEMORIES**

| EVENT | YEAR | EVENT | YEAR |
|---|---|---|---|
| | | | |
| | | | |
| | | | |

## OCTOBER 11

### BIRTHDAYS
| NAME | YEAR | NAME | YEAR |
|---|---|---|---|
| | | | |
| | | | |
| | | | |

### ANNIVERSARIES
| NAME | YEAR | NAME | YEAR |
|---|---|---|---|
| | | | |
| | | | |

### SPECIAL EVENTS & MEMORIES
| EVENT | YEAR | EVENT | YEAR |
|---|---|---|---|
| | | | |
| | | | |
| | | | |
| | | | |

## OCTOBER 12

### BIRTHDAYS
| NAME | YEAR | NAME | YEAR |
|---|---|---|---|
| | | | |
| | | | |
| | | | |

### ANNIVERSARIES
| NAME | YEAR | NAME | YEAR |
|---|---|---|---|
| | | | |
| | | | |

### SPECIAL EVENTS & MEMORIES
| EVENT | YEAR | EVENT | YEAR |
|---|---|---|---|
| | | | |
| | | | |
| | | | |
| | | | |

## OCTOBER 13

### BIRTHDAYS
| NAME | YEAR | NAME | YEAR |
|---|---|---|---|
| Ashley Hermance | | | |
| | | | |
| | | | |

### ANNIVERSARIES
| NAME | YEAR | NAME | YEAR |
|---|---|---|---|
| | | | |
| | | | |

### SPECIAL EVENTS & MEMORIES
| EVENT | YEAR | EVENT | YEAR |
|---|---|---|---|
| | | | |
| | | | |
| | | | |
| | | | |

# OCTOBER 14

**BIRTHDAYS**

| NAME | YEAR | NAME | YEAR |
|---|---|---|---|
| | | | |
| | | | |
| | | | |

**ANNIVERSARIES**

| NAME | YEAR | NAME | YEAR |
|---|---|---|---|
| | | | |
| | | | |

**SPECIAL EVENTS & MEMORIES**

| EVENT | YEAR | EVENT | YEAR |
|---|---|---|---|
| | | | |
| | | | |
| | | | |
| | | | |

# OCTOBER 15

**BIRTHDAYS**

| NAME | YEAR | NAME | YEAR |
|---|---|---|---|
| | | | |
| | | | |
| | | | |

**ANNIVERSARIES**

| NAME | YEAR | NAME | YEAR |
|---|---|---|---|
| | | | |
| | | | |

**SPECIAL EVENTS & MEMORIES**

| EVENT | YEAR | EVENT | YEAR |
|---|---|---|---|
| | | | |
| | | | |
| | | | |
| | | | |

# OCTOBER 16

**BIRTHDAYS**

| NAME | YEAR | NAME | YEAR |
|---|---|---|---|
| | | | |
| | | | |
| | | | |

**ANNIVERSARIES**

| NAME | YEAR | NAME | YEAR |
|---|---|---|---|
| | | | |
| | | | |

**SPECIAL EVENTS & MEMORIES**

| EVENT | YEAR | EVENT | YEAR |
|---|---|---|---|
| | | | |
| | | | |
| | | | |
| | | | |

## OCTOBER 17

### BIRTHDAYS
| NAME | YEAR | NAME | YEAR |
|---|---|---|---|
| Grandy! | | | |
| | | | |

### ANNIVERSARIES
| NAME | YEAR | NAME | YEAR |
|---|---|---|---|
| | | | |
| | | | |

### SPECIAL EVENTS & MEMORIES
| EVENT | YEAR | EVENT | YEAR |
|---|---|---|---|
| | | | |
| | | | |
| | | | |
| | | | |

## OCTOBER 18

### BIRTHDAYS
| NAME | YEAR | NAME | YEAR |
|---|---|---|---|
| | | | |
| | | | |

### ANNIVERSARIES
| NAME | YEAR | NAME | YEAR |
|---|---|---|---|
| | | | |
| | | | |

### SPECIAL EVENTS & MEMORIES
| EVENT | YEAR | EVENT | YEAR |
|---|---|---|---|
| | | | |
| | | | |
| | | | |
| | | | |

## OCTOBER 19

### BIRTHDAYS
| NAME | YEAR | NAME | YEAR |
|---|---|---|---|
| | | | |
| | | | |

### ANNIVERSARIES
| NAME | YEAR | NAME | YEAR |
|---|---|---|---|
| | | | |
| | | | |

### SPECIAL EVENTS & MEMORIES
| EVENT | YEAR | EVENT | YEAR |
|---|---|---|---|
| | | | |
| | | | |
| | | | |
| | | | |

# OCTOBER 20

**BIRTHDAYS**

| NAME | YEAR | NAME | YEAR |
|---|---|---|---|
| Emily Salerno | 1992 | | |
| | | | |

**ANNIVERSARIES**

| NAME | YEAR | NAME | YEAR |
|---|---|---|---|
| | | | |
| | | | |

**SPECIAL EVENTS & MEMORIES**

| EVENT | YEAR | EVENT | YEAR |
|---|---|---|---|
| | | | |
| | | | |
| | | | |

# OCTOBER 21

**BIRTHDAYS**

| NAME | YEAR | NAME | YEAR |
|---|---|---|---|
| Jack Stone | 2009 | | |
| | | | |

**ANNIVERSARIES**

| NAME | YEAR | NAME | YEAR |
|---|---|---|---|
| | | | |
| | | | |

**SPECIAL EVENTS & MEMORIES**

| EVENT | YEAR | EVENT | YEAR |
|---|---|---|---|
| | | | |
| | | | |
| | | | |

# OCTOBER 22

**BIRTHDAYS**

| NAME | YEAR | NAME | YEAR |
|---|---|---|---|
| | | | |
| | | | |

**ANNIVERSARIES**

| NAME | YEAR | NAME | YEAR |
|---|---|---|---|
| | | | |
| | | | |

**SPECIAL EVENTS & MEMORIES**

| EVENT | YEAR | EVENT | YEAR |
|---|---|---|---|
| | | | |
| | | | |
| | | | |

# OCTOBER 23

## BIRTHDAYS

| NAME | YEAR | NAME | YEAR |
|------|------|------|------|
|      |      |      |      |
|      |      |      |      |
|      |      |      |      |

## ANNIVERSARIES

| NAME | YEAR | NAME | YEAR |
|------|------|------|------|
|      |      |      |      |
|      |      |      |      |

## SPECIAL EVENTS & MEMORIES

| EVENT | YEAR | EVENT | YEAR |
|-------|------|-------|------|
|       |      |       |      |
|       |      |       |      |
|       |      |       |      |
|       |      |       |      |

# OCTOBER 24

## BIRTHDAYS

| NAME | YEAR | NAME | YEAR |
|------|------|------|------|
|      |      |      |      |
|      |      |      |      |
|      |      |      |      |

## ANNIVERSARIES

| NAME | YEAR | NAME | YEAR |
|------|------|------|------|
|      |      |      |      |
|      |      |      |      |

## SPECIAL EVENTS & MEMORIES

| EVENT | YEAR | EVENT | YEAR |
|-------|------|-------|------|
|       |      |       |      |
|       |      |       |      |
|       |      |       |      |
|       |      |       |      |

# OCTOBER 25

## BIRTHDAYS

| NAME | YEAR | NAME | YEAR |
|------|------|------|------|
|      |      |      |      |
|      |      |      |      |
|      |      |      |      |

## ANNIVERSARIES

| NAME | YEAR | NAME | YEAR |
|------|------|------|------|
|      |      |      |      |
|      |      |      |      |

## SPECIAL EVENTS & MEMORIES

| EVENT | YEAR | EVENT | YEAR |
|-------|------|-------|------|
|       |      |       |      |
|       |      |       |      |
|       |      |       |      |
|       |      |       |      |

# OCTOBER 26

**BIRTHDAYS**

| NAME | YEAR | NAME | YEAR |
|---|---|---|---|
| | | | |
| | | | |
| | | | |

**ANNIVERSARIES**

| NAME | YEAR | NAME | YEAR |
|---|---|---|---|
| | | | |
| | | | |

**SPECIAL EVENTS & MEMORIES**

| EVENT | YEAR | EVENT | YEAR |
|---|---|---|---|
| | | | |
| | | | |
| | | | |
| | | | |

# OCTOBER 27

**BIRTHDAYS**

| NAME | YEAR | NAME | YEAR |
|---|---|---|---|
| | | | |
| | | | |
| | | | |

**ANNIVERSARIES**

| NAME | YEAR | NAME | YEAR |
|---|---|---|---|
| | | | |
| | | | |

**SPECIAL EVENTS & MEMORIES**

| EVENT | YEAR | EVENT | YEAR |
|---|---|---|---|
| | | | |
| | | | |
| | | | |
| | | | |

# OCTOBER 28

**BIRTHDAYS**

| NAME | YEAR | NAME | YEAR |
|---|---|---|---|
| | | | |
| | | | |
| | | | |

**ANNIVERSARIES**

| NAME | YEAR | NAME | YEAR |
|---|---|---|---|
| | | | |
| | | | |

**SPECIAL EVENTS & MEMORIES**

| EVENT | YEAR | EVENT | YEAR |
|---|---|---|---|
| | | | |
| | | | |
| | | | |
| | | | |

# OCTOBER 29

## BIRTHDAYS

| NAME | YEAR | NAME | YEAR |
|---|---|---|---|
| Noah Bryant | 1997 | | |
| | | | |

## ANNIVERSARIES

| NAME | YEAR | NAME | YEAR |
|---|---|---|---|
| | | | |
| | | | |

## SPECIAL EVENTS & MEMORIES

| EVENT | YEAR | EVENT | YEAR |
|---|---|---|---|
| | | | |
| | | | |
| | | | |

# OCTOBER 30

## BIRTHDAYS

| NAME | YEAR | NAME | YEAR |
|---|---|---|---|
| | | | |
| | | | |

## ANNIVERSARIES

| NAME | YEAR | NAME | YEAR |
|---|---|---|---|
| | | | |
| | | | |

## SPECIAL EVENTS & MEMORIES

| EVENT | YEAR | EVENT | YEAR |
|---|---|---|---|
| | | | |
| | | | |
| | | | |

# OCTOBER 31

## BIRTHDAYS

| NAME | YEAR | NAME | YEAR |
|---|---|---|---|
| | | | |
| | | | |

## ANNIVERSARIES

| NAME | YEAR | NAME | YEAR |
|---|---|---|---|
| | | | |
| | | | |

## SPECIAL EVENTS & MEMORIES

| EVENT | YEAR | EVENT | YEAR |
|---|---|---|---|
| | | | |
| | | | |
| | | | |

# NOVEMBER

## NOVEMBER 1

### BIRTHDAYS

| NAME | YEAR | NAME | YEAR |
|------|------|------|------|
|  |  |  |  |
|  |  |  |  |
|  |  |  |  |

### ANNIVERSARIES

| NAME | YEAR | NAME | YEAR |
|------|------|------|------|
|  |  |  |  |
|  |  |  |  |

### SPECIAL EVENTS & MEMORIES

| EVENT | YEAR | EVENT | YEAR |
|-------|------|-------|------|
|  |  |  |  |
|  |  |  |  |
|  |  |  |  |
|  |  |  |  |

# NOVEMBER 2

### BIRTHDAYS
| NAME | YEAR | NAME | YEAR |
|---|---|---|---|
| | | | |
| | | | |

### ANNIVERSARIES
| NAME | YEAR | NAME | YEAR |
|---|---|---|---|
| | | | |

### SPECIAL EVENTS & MEMORIES
| EVENT | YEAR | EVENT | YEAR |
|---|---|---|---|
| | | | |
| | | | |
| | | | |

# NOVEMBER 3

### BIRTHDAYS
| NAME | YEAR | NAME | YEAR |
|---|---|---|---|
| | | | |
| | | | |

### ANNIVERSARIES
| NAME | YEAR | NAME | YEAR |
|---|---|---|---|
| | | | |

### SPECIAL EVENTS & MEMORIES
| EVENT | YEAR | EVENT | YEAR |
|---|---|---|---|
| | | | |
| | | | |
| | | | |

# NOVEMBER 4

### BIRTHDAYS
| NAME | YEAR | NAME | YEAR |
|---|---|---|---|
| | | | |
| | | | |

### ANNIVERSARIES
| NAME | YEAR | NAME | YEAR |
|---|---|---|---|
| | | | |

### SPECIAL EVENTS & MEMORIES
| EVENT | YEAR | EVENT | YEAR |
|---|---|---|---|
| | | | |
| | | | |
| | | | |

## NOVEMBER 5

### BIRTHDAYS
| NAME | YEAR | NAME | YEAR |
|---|---|---|---|
|  |  |  |  |
|  |  |  |  |
|  |  |  |  |

### ANNIVERSARIES
| NAME | YEAR | NAME | YEAR |
|---|---|---|---|
|  |  |  |  |
|  |  |  |  |

### SPECIAL EVENTS & MEMORIES
| EVENT | YEAR | EVENT | YEAR |
|---|---|---|---|
|  |  |  |  |
|  |  |  |  |
|  |  |  |  |
|  |  |  |  |

## NOVEMBER 6

### BIRTHDAYS
| NAME | YEAR | NAME | YEAR |
|---|---|---|---|
|  |  |  |  |
|  |  |  |  |
|  |  |  |  |

### ANNIVERSARIES
| NAME | YEAR | NAME | YEAR |
|---|---|---|---|
|  |  |  |  |
|  |  |  |  |

### SPECIAL EVENTS & MEMORIES
| EVENT | YEAR | EVENT | YEAR |
|---|---|---|---|
|  |  |  |  |
|  |  |  |  |
|  |  |  |  |
|  |  |  |  |

## NOVEMBER 7

### BIRTHDAYS
| NAME | YEAR | NAME | YEAR |
|---|---|---|---|
|  |  |  |  |
|  |  |  |  |
|  |  |  |  |

### ANNIVERSARIES
| NAME | YEAR | NAME | YEAR |
|---|---|---|---|
|  |  |  |  |
|  |  |  |  |

### SPECIAL EVENTS & MEMORIES
| EVENT | YEAR | EVENT | YEAR |
|---|---|---|---|
|  |  |  |  |
|  |  |  |  |
|  |  |  |  |
|  |  |  |  |

# NOVEMBER 8

## BIRTHDAYS

| NAME | YEAR | NAME | YEAR |
|---|---|---|---|
| | | | |
| | | | |
| | | | |

## ANNIVERSARIES

| NAME | YEAR | NAME | YEAR |
|---|---|---|---|
| | | | |
| | | | |

## SPECIAL EVENTS & MEMORIES

| EVENT | YEAR | EVENT | YEAR |
|---|---|---|---|
| | | | |
| | | | |
| | | | |
| | | | |

# NOVEMBER 9

## BIRTHDAYS

| NAME | YEAR | NAME | YEAR |
|---|---|---|---|
| | | | |
| | | | |
| | | | |

## ANNIVERSARIES

| NAME | YEAR | NAME | YEAR |
|---|---|---|---|
| | | | |
| | | | |

## SPECIAL EVENTS & MEMORIES

| EVENT | YEAR | EVENT | YEAR |
|---|---|---|---|
| | | | |
| | | | |
| | | | |
| | | | |

# NOVEMBER 10

## BIRTHDAYS

| NAME | YEAR | NAME | YEAR |
|---|---|---|---|
| | | | |
| | | | |
| | | | |

## ANNIVERSARIES

| NAME | YEAR | NAME | YEAR |
|---|---|---|---|
| | | | |
| | | | |

## SPECIAL EVENTS & MEMORIES

| EVENT | YEAR | EVENT | YEAR |
|---|---|---|---|
| | | | |
| | | | |
| | | | |
| | | | |

## NOVEMBER 11

### BIRTHDAYS

| NAME | YEAR | NAME | YEAR |
|---|---|---|---|
|  |  |  |  |
|  |  |  |  |
|  |  |  |  |

### ANNIVERSARIES

| NAME | YEAR | NAME | YEAR |
|---|---|---|---|
|  |  |  |  |
|  |  |  |  |

### SPECIAL EVENTS & MEMORIES

| EVENT | YEAR | EVENT | YEAR |
|---|---|---|---|
|  |  |  |  |
|  |  |  |  |
|  |  |  |  |
|  |  |  |  |

## NOVEMBER 12

### BIRTHDAYS

| NAME | YEAR | NAME | YEAR |
|---|---|---|---|
|  |  |  |  |
|  |  |  |  |
|  |  |  |  |

### ANNIVERSARIES

| NAME | YEAR | NAME | YEAR |
|---|---|---|---|
|  |  |  |  |
|  |  |  |  |

### SPECIAL EVENTS & MEMORIES

| EVENT | YEAR | EVENT | YEAR |
|---|---|---|---|
|  |  |  |  |
|  |  |  |  |
|  |  |  |  |
|  |  |  |  |

## NOVEMBER 13

### BIRTHDAYS

| NAME | YEAR | NAME | YEAR |
|---|---|---|---|
|  |  |  |  |
|  |  |  |  |
|  |  |  |  |

### ANNIVERSARIES

| NAME | YEAR | NAME | YEAR |
|---|---|---|---|
|  |  |  |  |
|  |  |  |  |

### SPECIAL EVENTS & MEMORIES

| EVENT | YEAR | EVENT | YEAR |
|---|---|---|---|
|  |  |  |  |
|  |  |  |  |
|  |  |  |  |
|  |  |  |  |

# NOVEMBER 14

**BIRTHDAYS**

| NAME | YEAR | NAME | YEAR |
|---|---|---|---|
| | | | |
| | | | |

**ANNIVERSARIES**

| NAME | YEAR | NAME | YEAR |
|---|---|---|---|
| | | | |
| | | | |

**SPECIAL EVENTS & MEMORIES**

| EVENT | YEAR | EVENT | YEAR |
|---|---|---|---|
| | | | |
| | | | |
| | | | |

# NOVEMBER 15

**BIRTHDAYS**

| NAME | YEAR | NAME | YEAR |
|---|---|---|---|
| | | | |
| | | | |

**ANNIVERSARIES**

| NAME | YEAR | NAME | YEAR |
|---|---|---|---|
| | | | |
| | | | |

**SPECIAL EVENTS & MEMORIES**

| EVENT | YEAR | EVENT | YEAR |
|---|---|---|---|
| | | | |
| | | | |
| | | | |

# NOVEMBER 16

**BIRTHDAYS**

| NAME | YEAR | NAME | YEAR |
|---|---|---|---|
| Gran-gran Bryant | 1942 | | |
| Brent Stone | | | |

**ANNIVERSARIES**

| NAME | YEAR | NAME | YEAR |
|---|---|---|---|
| | | | |
| | | | |

**SPECIAL EVENTS & MEMORIES**

| EVENT | YEAR | EVENT | YEAR |
|---|---|---|---|
| | | | |
| | | | |
| | | | |

# NOVEMBER 17

## BIRTHDAYS

| NAME | YEAR | NAME | YEAR |
|------|------|------|------|
|      |      |      |      |
|      |      |      |      |
|      |      |      |      |

## ANNIVERSARIES

| NAME | YEAR | NAME | YEAR |
|------|------|------|------|
|      |      |      |      |
|      |      |      |      |

## SPECIAL EVENTS & MEMORIES

| EVENT | YEAR | EVENT | YEAR |
|-------|------|-------|------|
|       |      |       |      |
|       |      |       |      |
|       |      |       |      |
|       |      |       |      |

# NOVEMBER 18

## BIRTHDAYS

| NAME | YEAR | NAME | YEAR |
|------|------|------|------|
|      |      |      |      |
|      |      |      |      |
|      |      |      |      |

## ANNIVERSARIES

| NAME | YEAR | NAME | YEAR |
|------|------|------|------|
|      |      |      |      |
|      |      |      |      |

## SPECIAL EVENTS & MEMORIES

| EVENT | YEAR | EVENT | YEAR |
|-------|------|-------|------|
|       |      |       |      |
|       |      |       |      |
|       |      |       |      |
|       |      |       |      |

# NOVEMBER 19

## BIRTHDAYS

| NAME | YEAR | NAME | YEAR |
|------|------|------|------|
|      |      |      |      |
|      |      |      |      |
|      |      |      |      |

## ANNIVERSARIES

| NAME | YEAR | NAME | YEAR |
|------|------|------|------|
|      |      |      |      |
|      |      |      |      |

## SPECIAL EVENTS & MEMORIES

| EVENT | YEAR | EVENT | YEAR |
|-------|------|-------|------|
|       |      |       |      |
|       |      |       |      |
|       |      |       |      |
|       |      |       |      |

# NOVEMBER 20

### BIRTHDAYS

| NAME | YEAR | NAME | YEAR |
|---|---|---|---|
| | | | |
| | | | |

### ANNIVERSARIES

| NAME | YEAR | NAME | YEAR |
|---|---|---|---|
| | | | |
| | | | |

### SPECIAL EVENTS & MEMORIES

| EVENT | YEAR | EVENT | YEAR |
|---|---|---|---|
| | | | |
| | | | |
| | | | |

# NOVEMBER 21

### BIRTHDAYS

| NAME | YEAR | NAME | YEAR |
|---|---|---|---|
| | | | |
| | | | |
| | | | |

### ANNIVERSARIES

| NAME | YEAR | NAME | YEAR |
|---|---|---|---|
| | | | |
| | | | |

### SPECIAL EVENTS & MEMORIES

| EVENT | YEAR | EVENT | YEAR |
|---|---|---|---|
| | | | |
| | | | |
| | | | |
| | | | |

# NOVEMBER 22

### BIRTHDAYS

| NAME | YEAR | NAME | YEAR |
|---|---|---|---|
| | | | |
| | | | |
| | | | |

### ANNIVERSARIES

| NAME | YEAR | NAME | YEAR |
|---|---|---|---|
| | | | |
| | | | |

### SPECIAL EVENTS & MEMORIES

| EVENT | YEAR | EVENT | YEAR |
|---|---|---|---|
| | | | |
| | | | |
| | | | |
| | | | |

## NOVEMBER 23

### BIRTHDAYS
| NAME | YEAR | NAME | YEAR |
|---|---|---|---|
| | | | |
| | | | |
| | | | |

### ANNIVERSARIES
| NAME | YEAR | NAME | YEAR |
|---|---|---|---|
| | | | |
| | | | |

### SPECIAL EVENTS & MEMORIES
| EVENT | YEAR | EVENT | YEAR |
|---|---|---|---|
| | | | |
| | | | |
| | | | |
| | | | |

## NOVEMBER 24

### BIRTHDAYS
| NAME | YEAR | NAME | YEAR |
|---|---|---|---|
| | | | |
| | | | |
| | | | |

### ANNIVERSARIES
| NAME | YEAR | NAME | YEAR |
|---|---|---|---|
| | | | |
| | | | |

### SPECIAL EVENTS & MEMORIES
| EVENT | YEAR | EVENT | YEAR |
|---|---|---|---|
| | | | |
| | | | |
| | | | |
| | | | |

## NOVEMBER 25

### BIRTHDAYS
| NAME | YEAR | NAME | YEAR |
|---|---|---|---|
| | | | |
| | | | |
| | | | |

### ANNIVERSARIES
| NAME | YEAR | NAME | YEAR |
|---|---|---|---|
| | | | |
| | | | |

### SPECIAL EVENTS & MEMORIES
| EVENT | YEAR | EVENT | YEAR |
|---|---|---|---|
| | | | |
| | | | |
| | | | |
| | | | |

# NOVEMBER 26

### BIRTHDAYS
| NAME | YEAR | NAME | YEAR |
|---|---|---|---|
| | | | |
| | | | |

### ANNIVERSARIES
| NAME | YEAR | NAME | YEAR |
|---|---|---|---|
| | | | |
| | | | |

### SPECIAL EVENTS & MEMORIES
| EVENT | YEAR | EVENT | YEAR |
|---|---|---|---|
| | | | |
| | | | |
| | | | |

# NOVEMBER 27

### BIRTHDAYS
| NAME | YEAR | NAME | YEAR |
|---|---|---|---|
| | | | |
| | | | |

### ANNIVERSARIES
| NAME | YEAR | NAME | YEAR |
|---|---|---|---|
| | | | |
| | | | |

### SPECIAL EVENTS & MEMORIES
| EVENT | YEAR | EVENT | YEAR |
|---|---|---|---|
| | | | |
| | | | |
| | | | |

# NOVEMBER 28

### BIRTHDAYS
| NAME | YEAR | NAME | YEAR |
|---|---|---|---|
| Harper Laura Elias | 2022 | | |
| Braedyn Robbins | | | |

### ANNIVERSARIES
| NAME | YEAR | NAME | YEAR |
|---|---|---|---|
| | | | |
| | | | |

### SPECIAL EVENTS & MEMORIES
| EVENT | YEAR | EVENT | YEAR |
|---|---|---|---|
| | | | |
| | | | |
| | | | |

# NOVEMBER 29

## BIRTHDAYS

| NAME | YEAR | NAME | YEAR |
|------|------|------|------|
|      |      |      |      |
|      |      |      |      |
|      |      |      |      |

## ANNIVERSARIES

| NAME | YEAR | NAME | YEAR |
|------|------|------|------|
|      |      |      |      |
|      |      |      |      |

## SPECIAL EVENTS & MEMORIES

| EVENT | YEAR | EVENT | YEAR |
|-------|------|-------|------|
|       |      |       |      |
|       |      |       |      |
|       |      |       |      |
|       |      |       |      |

# NOVEMBER 30

## BIRTHDAYS

| NAME | YEAR | NAME | YEAR |
|------|------|------|------|
|      |      |      |      |
|      |      |      |      |
|      |      |      |      |

## ANNIVERSARIES

| NAME | YEAR | NAME | YEAR |
|------|------|------|------|
|      |      |      |      |
|      |      |      |      |

## SPECIAL EVENTS & MEMORIES

| EVENT | YEAR | EVENT | YEAR |
|-------|------|-------|------|
|       |      |       |      |
|       |      |       |      |
|       |      |       |      |
|       |      |       |      |

## NOTES:

## DECEMBER 1

### BIRTHDAYS
| NAME | YEAR | NAME | YEAR |
|------|------|------|------|
|      |      |      |      |
|      |      |      |      |
|      |      |      |      |

### ANNIVERSARIES
| NAME | YEAR | NAME | YEAR |
|------|------|------|------|
|      |      |      |      |
|      |      |      |      |

### SPECIAL EVENTS & MEMORIES
| EVENT | YEAR | EVENT | YEAR |
|-------|------|-------|------|
|       |      |       |      |
|       |      |       |      |
|       |      |       |      |
|       |      |       |      |

# DECEMBER 2

**BIRTHDAYS**

| NAME | YEAR | NAME | YEAR |
|------|------|------|------|
|  |  |  |  |
|  |  |  |  |

**ANNIVERSARIES**

| NAME | YEAR | NAME | YEAR |
|------|------|------|------|
|  |  |  |  |
|  |  |  |  |

**SPECIAL EVENTS & MEMORIES**

| EVENT | YEAR | EVENT | YEAR |
|-------|------|-------|------|
|  |  |  |  |
|  |  |  |  |
|  |  |  |  |

# DECEMBER 3

**BIRTHDAYS**

| NAME | YEAR | NAME | YEAR |
|------|------|------|------|
|  |  |  |  |
|  |  |  |  |
|  |  |  |  |

**ANNIVERSARIES**

| NAME | YEAR | NAME | YEAR |
|------|------|------|------|
|  |  |  |  |
|  |  |  |  |

**SPECIAL EVENTS & MEMORIES**

| EVENT | YEAR | EVENT | YEAR |
|-------|------|-------|------|
|  |  |  |  |
|  |  |  |  |
|  |  |  |  |

# DECEMBER 4

**BIRTHDAYS**

| NAME | YEAR | NAME | YEAR |
|------|------|------|------|
| Lucy Costello | 2005 |  |  |
|  |  |  |  |

**ANNIVERSARIES**

| NAME | YEAR | NAME | YEAR |
|------|------|------|------|
|  |  |  |  |
|  |  |  |  |

**SPECIAL EVENTS & MEMORIES**

| EVENT | YEAR | EVENT | YEAR |
|-------|------|-------|------|
|  |  |  |  |
|  |  |  |  |
|  |  |  |  |

# DECEMBER 5

## BIRTHDAYS
| NAME | YEAR | NAME | YEAR |
|---|---|---|---|
|  |  |  |  |
|  |  |  |  |
|  |  |  |  |

## ANNIVERSARIES
| NAME | YEAR | NAME | YEAR |
|---|---|---|---|
|  |  |  |  |
|  |  |  |  |

## SPECIAL EVENTS & MEMORIES
| EVENT | YEAR | EVENT | YEAR |
|---|---|---|---|
|  |  |  |  |
|  |  |  |  |
|  |  |  |  |
|  |  |  |  |

# DECEMBER 6

## BIRTHDAYS
| NAME | YEAR | NAME | YEAR |
|---|---|---|---|
|  |  |  |  |
|  |  |  |  |
|  |  |  |  |

## ANNIVERSARIES
| NAME | YEAR | NAME | YEAR |
|---|---|---|---|
|  |  |  |  |
|  |  |  |  |

## SPECIAL EVENTS & MEMORIES
| EVENT | YEAR | EVENT | YEAR |
|---|---|---|---|
|  |  |  |  |
|  |  |  |  |
|  |  |  |  |
|  |  |  |  |

# DECEMBER 7

## BIRTHDAYS
| NAME | YEAR | NAME | YEAR |
|---|---|---|---|
|  |  |  |  |
|  |  |  |  |
|  |  |  |  |

## ANNIVERSARIES
| NAME | YEAR | NAME | YEAR |
|---|---|---|---|
|  |  |  |  |
|  |  |  |  |

## SPECIAL EVENTS & MEMORIES
| EVENT | YEAR | EVENT | YEAR |
|---|---|---|---|
|  |  |  |  |
|  |  |  |  |
|  |  |  |  |
|  |  |  |  |

# DECEMBER 8

**BIRTHDAYS**

| NAME | YEAR | NAME | YEAR |
|---|---|---|---|
| Abby Bryant | 2001 | | |
| | | | |

**ANNIVERSARIES**

| NAME | YEAR | NAME | YEAR |
|---|---|---|---|
| | | | |
| | | | |

**SPECIAL EVENTS & MEMORIES**

| EVENT | YEAR | EVENT | YEAR |
|---|---|---|---|
| | | | |
| | | | |
| | | | |

# DECEMBER 9

**BIRTHDAYS**

| NAME | YEAR | NAME | YEAR |
|---|---|---|---|
| | | | |
| | | | |

**ANNIVERSARIES**

| NAME | YEAR | NAME | YEAR |
|---|---|---|---|
| | | | |
| | | | |

**SPECIAL EVENTS & MEMORIES**

| EVENT | YEAR | EVENT | YEAR |
|---|---|---|---|
| | | | |
| | | | |
| | | | |

# DECEMBER 10

**BIRTHDAYS**

| NAME | YEAR | NAME | YEAR |
|---|---|---|---|
| | | | |
| | | | |

**ANNIVERSARIES**

| NAME | YEAR | NAME | YEAR |
|---|---|---|---|
| | | | |
| | | | |

**SPECIAL EVENTS & MEMORIES**

| EVENT | YEAR | EVENT | YEAR |
|---|---|---|---|
| | | | |
| | | | |
| | | | |

## DECEMBER 11

### BIRTHDAYS
| NAME | YEAR | NAME | YEAR |
|---|---|---|---|
|  |  |  |  |
|  |  |  |  |
|  |  |  |  |

### ANNIVERSARIES
| NAME | YEAR | NAME | YEAR |
|---|---|---|---|
|  |  |  |  |
|  |  |  |  |

### SPECIAL EVENTS & MEMORIES
| EVENT | YEAR | EVENT | YEAR |
|---|---|---|---|
|  |  |  |  |
|  |  |  |  |
|  |  |  |  |
|  |  |  |  |

## DECEMBER 12

### BIRTHDAYS
| NAME | YEAR | NAME | YEAR |
|---|---|---|---|
|  |  |  |  |
|  |  |  |  |
|  |  |  |  |

### ANNIVERSARIES
| NAME | YEAR | NAME | YEAR |
|---|---|---|---|
|  |  |  |  |
|  |  |  |  |

### SPECIAL EVENTS & MEMORIES
| EVENT | YEAR | EVENT | YEAR |
|---|---|---|---|
|  |  |  |  |
|  |  |  |  |
|  |  |  |  |
|  |  |  |  |

## DECEMBER 13

### BIRTHDAYS
| NAME | YEAR | NAME | YEAR |
|---|---|---|---|
|  |  |  |  |
|  |  |  |  |
|  |  |  |  |

### ANNIVERSARIES
| NAME | YEAR | NAME | YEAR |
|---|---|---|---|
|  |  |  |  |
|  |  |  |  |

### SPECIAL EVENTS & MEMORIES
| EVENT | YEAR | EVENT | YEAR |
|---|---|---|---|
|  |  |  |  |
|  |  |  |  |
|  |  |  |  |
|  |  |  |  |

# DECEMBER 14

## BIRTHDAYS

| NAME | YEAR | NAME | YEAR |
|---|---|---|---|
| | | | |
| | | | |
| | | | |

## ANNIVERSARIES

| NAME | YEAR | NAME | YEAR |
|---|---|---|---|
| | | | |
| | | | |

## SPECIAL EVENTS & MEMORIES

| EVENT | YEAR | EVENT | YEAR |
|---|---|---|---|
| | | | |
| | | | |
| | | | |
| | | | |

# DECEMBER 15

## BIRTHDAYS

| NAME | YEAR | NAME | YEAR |
|---|---|---|---|
| | | | |
| | | | |
| | | | |

## ANNIVERSARIES

| NAME | YEAR | NAME | YEAR |
|---|---|---|---|
| | | | |
| | | | |

## SPECIAL EVENTS & MEMORIES

| EVENT | YEAR | EVENT | YEAR |
|---|---|---|---|
| | | | |
| | | | |
| | | | |
| | | | |

# DECEMBER 16

## BIRTHDAYS

| NAME | YEAR | NAME | YEAR |
|---|---|---|---|
| | | | |
| | | | |
| | | | |

## ANNIVERSARIES

| NAME | YEAR | NAME | YEAR |
|---|---|---|---|
| | | | |
| | | | |

## SPECIAL EVENTS & MEMORIES

| EVENT | YEAR | EVENT | YEAR |
|---|---|---|---|
| | | | |
| | | | |
| | | | |
| | | | |

# DECEMBER 17

## BIRTHDAYS

| NAME | YEAR | NAME | YEAR |
|------|------|------|------|
|      |      |      |      |
|      |      |      |      |
|      |      |      |      |

## ANNIVERSARIES

| NAME | YEAR | NAME | YEAR |
|------|------|------|------|
|      |      |      |      |
|      |      |      |      |

## SPECIAL EVENTS & MEMORIES

| EVENT | YEAR | EVENT | YEAR |
|-------|------|-------|------|
|       |      |       |      |
|       |      |       |      |
|       |      |       |      |
|       |      |       |      |

# DECEMBER 18

## BIRTHDAYS

| NAME | YEAR | NAME | YEAR |
|------|------|------|------|
|      |      |      |      |
|      |      |      |      |
|      |      |      |      |

## ANNIVERSARIES

| NAME | YEAR | NAME | YEAR |
|------|------|------|------|
|      |      |      |      |
|      |      |      |      |

## SPECIAL EVENTS & MEMORIES

| EVENT | YEAR | EVENT | YEAR |
|-------|------|-------|------|
|       |      |       |      |
|       |      |       |      |
|       |      |       |      |
|       |      |       |      |

# DECEMBER 19

## BIRTHDAYS

| NAME | YEAR | NAME | YEAR |
|------|------|------|------|
|      |      |      |      |
|      |      |      |      |
|      |      |      |      |

## ANNIVERSARIES

| NAME | YEAR | NAME | YEAR |
|------|------|------|------|
|      |      |      |      |
|      |      |      |      |

## SPECIAL EVENTS & MEMORIES

| EVENT | YEAR | EVENT | YEAR |
|-------|------|-------|------|
|       |      |       |      |
|       |      |       |      |
|       |      |       |      |
|       |      |       |      |

## DECEMBER 20

**BIRTHDAYS**

| NAME | YEAR | NAME | YEAR |
|------|------|------|------|
|      |      |      |      |
|      |      |      |      |

**ANNIVERSARIES**

| NAME | YEAR | NAME | YEAR |
|------|------|------|------|
|      |      |      |      |
|      |      |      |      |

**SPECIAL EVENTS & MEMORIES**

| EVENT | YEAR | EVENT | YEAR |
|-------|------|-------|------|
|       |      |       |      |
|       |      |       |      |
|       |      |       |      |

## DECEMBER 21

**BIRTHDAYS**

| NAME | YEAR | NAME | YEAR |
|------|------|------|------|
|      |      |      |      |
|      |      |      |      |

**ANNIVERSARIES**

| NAME | YEAR | NAME | YEAR |
|------|------|------|------|
|      |      |      |      |
|      |      |      |      |

**SPECIAL EVENTS & MEMORIES**

| EVENT | YEAR | EVENT | YEAR |
|-------|------|-------|------|
|       |      |       |      |
|       |      |       |      |
|       |      |       |      |

## DECEMBER 22

**BIRTHDAYS**

| NAME | YEAR | NAME | YEAR |
|------|------|------|------|
| Evans Elliott | 1997 |  |  |
|      |      |      |      |

**ANNIVERSARIES**

| NAME | YEAR | NAME | YEAR |
|------|------|------|------|
|      |      |      |      |
|      |      |      |      |

**SPECIAL EVENTS & MEMORIES**

| EVENT | YEAR | EVENT | YEAR |
|-------|------|-------|------|
|       |      |       |      |
|       |      |       |      |
|       |      |       |      |

# DECEMBER 23

## BIRTHDAYS
| NAME | YEAR | NAME | YEAR |
|---|---|---|---|
| | | | |
| | | | |
| | | | |

## ANNIVERSARIES
| NAME | YEAR | NAME | YEAR |
|---|---|---|---|
| | | | |
| | | | |

## SPECIAL EVENTS & MEMORIES
| EVENT | YEAR | EVENT | YEAR |
|---|---|---|---|
| | | | |
| | | | |
| | | | |
| | | | |

# DECEMBER 24

## BIRTHDAYS
| NAME | YEAR | NAME | YEAR |
|---|---|---|---|
| Moraya Gavin | | | |
| Krista Mallon | | | |
| | | | |

## ANNIVERSARIES
| NAME | YEAR | NAME | YEAR |
|---|---|---|---|
| | | | |
| | | | |

## SPECIAL EVENTS & MEMORIES
| EVENT | YEAR | EVENT | YEAR |
|---|---|---|---|
| | | | |
| | | | |
| | | | |
| | | | |

# DECEMBER 25

## BIRTHDAYS
| NAME | YEAR | NAME | YEAR |
|---|---|---|---|
| | | | |
| | | | |
| | | | |

## ANNIVERSARIES
| NAME | YEAR | NAME | YEAR |
|---|---|---|---|
| | | | |
| | | | |

## SPECIAL EVENTS & MEMORIES
| EVENT | YEAR | EVENT | YEAR |
|---|---|---|---|
| | | | |
| | | | |
| | | | |
| | | | |

# DECEMBER 26

**BIRTHDAYS**

| NAME | YEAR | NAME | YEAR |
|---|---|---|---|
|  |  |  |  |
|  |  |  |  |
|  |  |  |  |

**ANNIVERSARIES**

| NAME | YEAR | NAME | YEAR |
|---|---|---|---|
|  |  |  |  |
|  |  |  |  |

**SPECIAL EVENTS & MEMORIES**

| EVENT | YEAR | EVENT | YEAR |
|---|---|---|---|
|  |  |  |  |
|  |  |  |  |
|  |  |  |  |
|  |  |  |  |

# DECEMBER 27

**BIRTHDAYS**

| NAME | YEAR | NAME | YEAR |
|---|---|---|---|
|  |  |  |  |
|  |  |  |  |
|  |  |  |  |

**ANNIVERSARIES**

| NAME | YEAR | NAME | YEAR |
|---|---|---|---|
|  |  |  |  |
|  |  |  |  |

**SPECIAL EVENTS & MEMORIES**

| EVENT | YEAR | EVENT | YEAR |
|---|---|---|---|
|  |  |  |  |
|  |  |  |  |
|  |  |  |  |
|  |  |  |  |

# DECEMBER 28

**BIRTHDAYS**

| NAME | YEAR | NAME | YEAR |
|---|---|---|---|
|  |  |  |  |
|  |  |  |  |
|  |  |  |  |

**ANNIVERSARIES**

| NAME | YEAR | NAME | YEAR |
|---|---|---|---|
|  |  |  |  |
|  |  |  |  |

**SPECIAL EVENTS & MEMORIES**

| EVENT | YEAR | EVENT | YEAR |
|---|---|---|---|
|  |  |  |  |
|  |  |  |  |
|  |  |  |  |
|  |  |  |  |

## DECEMBER 29

**BIRTHDAYS**

| NAME | YEAR | NAME | YEAR |
|---|---|---|---|
| Olivia Toledano | 1997 | | |
| | | | |
| | | | |

**ANNIVERSARIES**

| NAME | YEAR | NAME | YEAR |
|---|---|---|---|
| | | | |
| | | | |

**SPECIAL EVENTS & MEMORIES**

| EVENT | YEAR | EVENT | YEAR |
|---|---|---|---|
| | | | |
| | | | |
| | | | |

## DECEMBER 30

**BIRTHDAYS**

| NAME | YEAR | NAME | YEAR |
|---|---|---|---|
| | | | |
| | | | |
| | | | |

**ANNIVERSARIES**

| NAME | YEAR | NAME | YEAR |
|---|---|---|---|
| | | | |
| | | | |

**SPECIAL EVENTS & MEMORIES**

| EVENT | YEAR | EVENT | YEAR |
|---|---|---|---|
| | | | |
| | | | |
| | | | |

## DECEMBER 31

**BIRTHDAYS**

| NAME | YEAR | NAME | YEAR |
|---|---|---|---|
| Bernie Olszeski | 1965 | | |
| | | | |
| | | | |

**ANNIVERSARIES**

| NAME | YEAR | NAME | YEAR |
|---|---|---|---|
| | | | |
| | | | |

**SPECIAL EVENTS & MEMORIES**

| EVENT | YEAR | EVENT | YEAR |
|---|---|---|---|
| | | | |
| | | | |
| | | | |

NOTES

# NOTES

# NOTES

# NOTES

# NOTES

# NOTES

Made in the USA
Columbia, SC
13 December 2022

f7cd73bb-dcd3-43f7-94f4-7946f6fb4933R01